DO *EVERYTHING* THEY TELL YOU *NOT* TO DO... IF YOU WANT TO SUCCEED

DO *EVERYTHING* THEY TELL YOU *NOT* TO DO...
IF YOU WANT TO SUCCEED

FURTHERING THE ART OF PERSISTENCE

SANJAY BURMAN

BURMANBOOKS

Cover and interior design:
Jack Steiner Graphic Design

Editing:
Kimberlee MacDonald

Distribution:
Trumedia Group
c/o Ingram Publisher Services
14 Ingram Blvd.
LaVergne, TN 37086

ISBN 978-1-897404-04-1

Dedication

I must thank Dr. William Prusin, John Manikaros, Kimberlee MacDonald and Dory Benami (whose name was spelled incorrectly in the last book), and most importantly, you the readers... well, Alyssa Milano and Anne Hathaway too.

Seriously, I get no greater pleasure than having readers tell me the results of following the exercises in the book, overcoming their fears and moving forward with their lives, keeping in mind I have never had the pleasure of Ms. Milano or Ms. Hathaway's company.

Table of Contents

Chapter 1   Don't Be Afraid (except of Shirley MacLaine *1*

Chapter 2   Be Creative *24*

Chapter 3   Step Up and Make It Happen *29*

Chapter 4   Don't Take 'No' *40*

Chapter 5   Earn Respect, Don't Expect Respect *50*

Chapter 6   Don't Burn Bridges, Unless It Can't Be Helped *60*

Chapter 7   Fewer "Yes" Men *71*

Chapter 8   Shut Up! And Be Truthful To Yourself *80*

Chapter 9   Opportunities Knock *87*

Chapter 10   Endear Yourself To Others *97*

Chapter 11   What To Do When Someone Says Yes! *102*

Fear Journal *106*

If your problem has a solution, why worry about it? If your problem has no solution, why worry about it?

CHINESE PROVERB

Chapter 1:

Don't Be Afraid (except of Shirley MacLaine)

How to make fear work for you

Let's clear the decks first. Some fears are healthy—like of large animals with sharp teeth, Shirley MacLaine (I'll get to that later in the book, I promise!) or possibly, your in-laws. While that might stop you from, say, climbing into the lion enclosure at the zoo, or the potentially more terrifying prospect of your spouse's family reunion—both legitimate in their own way—most of our fears do little more than stunt our potential and keep us from growing.

It is, without a doubt, the biggest barrier to our own success. It's not procrastination. It's not fate. It's nothing more than plain, simple fear. You know you have it; we all do. Despite the various cliffs I've jumped off, I've got a dose of it, too. I've just taken some time to see fears for what they are: 90% of them are unhealthy hurdles developed by your conscious mind to guard your unconscious from looking stupid, offending others or breaking a value system.

Fear is an emotion developed by your ego and we know how destructive that can be. Look closely now and call it what it is: When we need to get the last word in, that's your ego talking;

if we sulk when we don't get something, or immediately find flaws in a person that rejected us, that's our dented egos, pushing back. That's where it comes from: The overriding fear we all have of looking weak or vulnerable. That's what stops us from achieving true power and freedom.

Make sense? No? Don't worry. The brain is a complex landscape, one with all sorts of conforming influences. Conforming to society goes all the way back to Adam and Eve. We want to be rich, famous and happy and anyone who tells you they're happy without money is lying; they've just convinced themselves it can't happen to them. We're just too afraid to go for it. Why? We're told from day one that it's not something a 'normal person' can achieve. We think only the Trumps, or Blacks are the ones born with that 'luck'.

Show me a lucky millionaire and I'll show you a billionaire who went broke three times before he hit it big. Why? He wasn't afraid to try. Most importantly: He wasn't afraid to fail and try again.

So what's your excuse now? If you can contain your ego and balance your fear, I'll show you the next step to your dreams.

I'm constantly coaching people past their fears. I've listed a few examples below. It's funny; each time, almost without fail, I hear the same thing at the outset: "I really want to become successful and I disagree with you: I don't have an ego and I'm not afraid of success." Afterwards, it's always the same response: 'Wow, I didn't know I had that fear or ego problem!"

GET OUT OF YOUR FREAKING COMFORT ZONE!!!

If there is only one thing I would like to see happen as a motivational speaker/author, it's to see you all get out of your comfort zone (in case you missed the caps in the heading). When I'm doing one-on-one consulting with people, I have them do one thing a day that scares them. We need to push ourselves to grow. We need to feel rejection to understand that it's not the end of the world, or even a second thought 30 seconds later. The Japanese have a great saying that the grass that is long is weak and dies the first time someone walks on it, but the short grass that's always crushed by feet, grows stronger.

I remember going to a club with a few friends some years back. I really didn't want to go; I was never into that scene since I don't drink and watching me dance is like watching someone having a seizure. But I agreed to go anyway. The minute we got there, a waitress approached me and said that a girl on the other side of the bar was buying me a diet coke. My friends were as impressed as I was. As I began to sip my new drink, the waitress returned, 'I'm sorry, but the girl meant that for someone else.' To add insult to injury, she even took the drink away from me! I mean come on! I had already taken a sip, for God's sake! My friends ignored my begging to go home and we proceeded further into the club. Just as we had taken another 10 steps, security mistook me for someone else and pinned me against the wall. Ok, this was not going to be a good night.

After that incident was cleared up, I was sitting at a table and I noticed a very pretty girl with her friends. She was obviously a regular, since she appeared to know everyone, but she had my eye. My friends kept trying to convince me to go and speak to her. I was way too nervous. She was with her friends and I'm not comfortable with just walking up to a girl like that. Finally, close to the end of the night, I saw her pass by our table on her own. My friends pushed me from behind, so I started to try and catch up to her. As we got to a crowd of people, she was wading through them and I figured she was getting close to her friends; this was my last opportunity. So I raised my hand to tap her on the shoulder. As I did, she suddenly turned her head to talk to someone and my fingers got trapped in her hair. I pulled my hand back and with it, came her head. I freaked out as I saw this potential whip lash victim! I turned to the tall guy beside me and said, 'Why'd you do that?' He just looked at me with a pathetic rolling of the eyes. She looked back at me with hatred in hers and I figured this was as good a time as and said, "Hi, I saw you earlier tonight. How are you?" She turned and walked away.

The point of this story, other than giving away too much information, is that her rejection didn't change my life; therefore it hasn't affected me. It was a little embarrassing or even painful at the time, but by the time I'd gotten home that night, I had almost forgotten the whole thing.

On another note, I had bad experience after bad experience with directing. So I convinced myself I was a bad director and hired others. Finally, the day came when I had no choice but to direct *The Search for the Balanced Life.* Bruce, my lawyer had basically forced me to do it due to time constraints and the fact that I was the only one who knew what the end product should be. The first part of it was bad, but then as I kept going, it got better and better. Today, I'm no longer afraid to step into the director's chair and tell the story myself. I don't get an opportunity to do so as often, since I'm producing movies, TV shows, publishing books and speaking to audiences. But the fact that I'm not scared is what has taken a lot of weight off of my shoulders. Try it.

Try following these exercises. If they seem risky, that's because they are. But I won't ask you to do anything embarrassing or painful (because I want you to buy my next book, as well). Just have some faith and you'll see how your thinking can change forever.

The Art of the Cold Call

One of the hardest things to do is approach someone blind—no introduction, no appointment, just ice cold. It's a feature of our personal and professional lives: A friend we want to reconnect with, a person we want to date or someone with power we want to hit up for a job, a sale or a favour.

But some people make their living at it: Telemarketers—a tough, tough job if there ever was one—or real estate agents, who cold call for new listing potentials. An older example is the door-to-door salesman, who sold anything from encyclopaedias to vacuum cleaners. Not easy. But you have to remember what you're really selling: Yourself.

I know; I've done it lots of times. Any time I had to raise money, get a team together or ask for someone's help, people would always bet on me. They can't see the future any better than I can; they don't know if it's going to be successful. But they can tell that I'm worth the bet. Now look at yourself: If you were regarded the same way you regard yourself, would *you* bet on *you*?

Most people would say no. There's good reason. They're afraid.

The cold call mentality has to be right for you to deal with it properly. You can't have a high school mentality, where you're afraid you'll make a fool of yourself and be branded by the other kids; it's not personal. The people on the receiving end want you to make their lives better! They don't want to make your life worse.

Think about it. Here's a tough example: A polished encyclopaedia salesman rarely offers the deal to the homeowner up front. He or she will quickly ask if there are children in the house. If it's yes, they go for it: Not only is it a great gift, but it's a brilliant educational resource for school projects, general interest and expanding the child's knowledge. The salesman has turned what might be seen as an unnecessary expense into a valuable investment!

See your cold call from your subject's point of view, not yours. How would you respond to this pitch? "Would you like to buy this? It's a beautiful encyclopaedia series. It's also really cheap, today only." That has nothing to do with you. Should you buy a truck load of women's bras because they're cheap? Get into your subject's head: Determine what they get out of the deal, and let them know how and why their life is better with your product than without it.

You should apply this to every aspect of your life. Your brain is wired for survival. As a result, we're always sensitized to how any situation benefits us. Some are a little more hardwired than others, which can lead to selfishness (just look at some of the women I've dated), but let's not complicate things, shall we?

It was a truly important cold call that gave my business some breathing room. It was with Bob Proctor. When I was in high school, the best known motivational speaker was Anthony Robbins. He was like a rock star in the motivational world. However, for my father's generation, it was Bob Proctor. He made a huge entry into my generation with The Secret. I wasn't sure what to think of him based on the movie, but I knew that he was very formal looking and brought history with him. I had put quite a bit of effort into getting him.

It started with my emailing a generic email address that of course received no response. I was at a signing with Marie Diamond, and someone came up to us and said that he was sent from Bob Proctor's office just to pay his respects to her. I quickly gave him a business card and told him that we wanted to publish Mr. Proctor. No response.

Ok, I like the whole 'hard to get' game too.

There was a journalist whom I got along with and he started to follow Mr. Proctor and wrote several articles about him. I got my in. I got together with the journalist and told him that I would give him an exclusive if he gave me the home phone number for Bob Proctor. It actually worked! As nervous as he was in giving it to me, he thought of his career and also was reassured by my promise that I would never tell who gave me the number.

I phoned Mr. Proctor's home every day for a week until he finally gave me the time of day. He told me he was busy and that I should call back seven days from then. I did; then another seven days and another. It went on for three weeks. Finally, he suggested that I meet him for breakfast. So we finally met face to face.

We met a further three times. The one thing I knew was that Mr. Proctor loved my persistence. He may have been annoyed at times, but in all sincerity, I didn't care since he was someone who would sell a lot of books and I wanted to make my business a success by being around successful people. It turns out, that he actually liked my style and encouraged it. The more I pushed, the more he would accommodate me; even with a busy schedule. For instance, I thanked him for doing the book with us, but then said, 'it's too bad we have no time to promote it with you.' He looked at me and asked what I had in mind. I said I would have loved to do a Christmas tour with him, across North America. He agreed to tour for one week. His team wasn't too happy with such a large commitment.

If you've set your sights on something, focus and go after it. If you piss the person off, pull back a bit and then proceed in again. Most people won't get upset. Those who do are feeling threatened and therefore it's not personal.

So I signed Bob Proctor to a book deal; cause for celebration, you'd think. But I was in deep trouble. I didn't have the money to pull it off! So, again, I had to be creative and think outside the box.

I had just moved into a very expensive neighbourhood on the waterfront and my rent was steep. I told my father and my lawyer, Bruce, that I was going to attempt to negotiate with my landlord for a year's free rent. The funny part is, even with all the things I've accomplished in my life, neither of them was optimistic about my chances.

I took my landlord out to dinner and told him that since I thought he was a gambler (had no idea), I thought this was something that might interest him; he would either win big, or lose 12 months rent. I offered him 2% of the profits from Proctor's book in lieu of my rent for a year. Potentially, this meant that he could not only make more than what the rent would have been, but he'd maybe be getting a cheque for the next five years!

He thought about it and an hour later, he agreed. I say this to people over and over: The simplest solution is often the best! However, most people think that it's so simple, either someone else has done it, or they wouldn't go for it because it's too simple and stupid. Most of us use a past experience to dictate the results of a future action. Yet, when I'm in a one-on-one consultation, I will urge the person to go and do the thing they think they know the answer to. For instance, 'I can't tell my parents; they got mad before.'; 'I can't ask for a raise; he said no before.' Well, if you know the answer, then you really have nothing to lose. But, if you're surprised by a different result, you're further ahead!

That's just one such story in my life. My father and my lawyer have both seen it all; watching with amazement. But the Proctor situation shocked them. This was a big, big name; I knew I couldn't let him go. I wouldn't be stopped, but I had to contain my emotions. If my landlord knew how badly I needed the money for my business to flourish, he would have seen my desperation, smelled my fear and been scared off.

What I showed him instead was how 'we' could flourish. I think he's going to do very well with his gamble. Bob Proctor is a huge speaker and has been for a long time. I don't want to call it a slam dunk, but if we do our job to the best of our abilities, it should be a bestselling book.

The second thing about cold calling is that you need to control your own insecurities. Don't think of yourself as being judged. People are too busy to care about a salesman they just turned down. When they hang up or close the door, it's not even a second thought; they've forgotten you. So who cares if they say no? We'll talk about what a no actually is further in.

Finally, a cold call can open possibilities that you didn't see before! In a hero's journey, the hero is on a path to complete a task. However, the hero will sometimes deviate to find out more information from an aide. Your aide is your potential sale.

I have been in situations where I think I know what I'm selling, but after listening to what someone really wants, I find I'm able to tailor the product to suit the market's needs: "I don't want what you're offering," I've heard people say, "But if you were to make it more of this, then I'd be interested and so would many others." This tip is a keeper! Now you've learned from someone what you need to do to make them say 'yes.' This information is invaluable.

All successful people will tailor their services to fit the market, whether that's a niche or mass market. Stop talking and start listening! Listen to people; if you're willing to listen, they'll tell you all you need to know—their likes, dislikes, fears and dreams. That goes double for your personal life. Keep an ear out. It'll serve you well.

When I directed *The Search for the Balanced Life*, I did what I thought was a humorous take on a serious subject (I believe we all need to laugh more). At first, I stuck to my guns and wouldn't change it. Finally, I showed it to several people who all told me the same thing: Change it! So I did. Because I listened, it became a success and reached more people than it could have if I had been stubborn.

A 'no' is a temporary response to a long-term solution

No is not a bad word. In fact, it's a great word. You have to be told 'no' before you reel in the 'yes.' A person says 'no' not because he or she doesn't want what you're offering. They say 'no' because they don't know they want it! YOU have to show them how it can benefit them. Be passionate, not arrogant. Be excited, not selfish. Be creative, but don't lie.

My guess is that I have heard 'no' 500,000 times and about 2,000 yeses. The yeses got me to where I am. The answer 'no' prepared me to get there. Don't think about a 'no' as personal. If someone takes the time to say no, ask them why. Even a response like, 'I just don't need it,' or 'it's just not of interest to me,' can tell you a lot! It means you've got more work to do to tailor your product to their needs or interests. Once you do that, you've covered some important ground: You've taken important steps forward and you're prepared for the future!

Athletes always try new techniques when they're training; knowing full well they will fall flat the first few times. They do it through training sessions for obvious reasons. Getting a 'no' is your training session. Don't be afraid of your mistakes. Learn from them. The more you do, the more you will get over your fear and ego.

It's also important to keep emotion out. When you are told 'no', don't get mad or sulk. When my parents first started their printing business, my father had to make cold calls to potential customers. My father is a soft-hearted man and rejection was difficult for him. He saw a 'no' as a rejection. He took it personally. It took several of them and some time for him to understand that the people who said 'no' to him didn't even know him—it was just business!

Eventually, he would get a 'no' and then follow up with, "Why?" He would go back to the office and a few weeks later go back to the same customer and armed with the information his 'why' had yielded, re-pitch himself and get a 'yes'!

Go out and get a 'no'. It's good for you!

Insecurities are your friend … in hell!

Insecurities aren't always obvious. Successful people know how to read others; they can detect insecurities by reading 'between the lines'. We preach what we must learn. I always tell people, when they hear someone say, "I'm an honest person; I'm always fair," *run*! Run as fast as you can! Honest people don't need to tell you they are honest, they show it by BEING honest.

Your mother probably told you actions speak louder than words. It's very true. When someone makes an appointment to come and see me, I start with a very long conversation. I love to hear them speak about the beliefs they think they follow. I let them go on and on—honesty, lack of fear, unselfishness and so on. Those people are trying to convince themselves of something they're not!

My only advice to you is that now you have the information about that person, you can use it to sell yourself or product. By repeating back to them what they just said, you calm their insecurities and feed their ego. If someone tells you about how honest they are, you have an opening to exploit: "Knowing what an honest person you are, I knew I had to speak to you about this matter."

We all have insecurities. You have them because you've chosen to live a fantasy. What we need to do is accept and control them. I'll give you an example. I was out to dinner with a woman recently and she started to cry about a past memory that had hurt her badly. I had known from the first day I met her that she was running from something in particular, but I hadn't felt the need to bring it up until it came up on its own, four months later.

She cried at the table in the restaurant and excused herself. I took her out to the parking lot and hugged her. She finally calmed down and was quiet. I asked her why she was quiet; she was afraid that I would abandon her.

Before we go any further, try reading between the lines. What caused her insecurity? It's not hard to guess: She had been left before. I'm sure you got it. As your winning gift, you get this book!

Where did this insecurity come from? It was a fantasy. Her response was that "people don't like weakness." She also said, "you aren't supposed to show weakness." These are fantasies created by assumptions that lead to fears.

Whenever you use words like 'shouldn't', 'couldn't', 'supposed to' or anything else that invokes societal expectations, you're reducing yourself, making yourself inferior. That's what happens when you compare yourself to something or someone out of your reach.

If that's the only level that's acceptable to you, then anything less is failure. Not true. This is why they put blinders on racehorses. If a horse was to see all the confusion of other horses running beside it, it would get excited and run in circles. This way, the horse can only see the finish line and aim for it. Technically, the horse is only competing with itself.

My friend and fellow author Dr. John Demartini talks about this in *The Gratitude Effect*. He says that for the great life you think someone has, look closer. You will see that they don't have what you have! They may have money and fame, but lack happiness and true friendships. You may have a great car, but lack a great marriage. The balance keeps us striving for more out of life.

It's when you compare yourself to others that you get into the 'dog chasing the tail' theory. I loved whipping my dog's face with his own tail and then watching him spin around forever, trying to chase it! It provided many moments of entertainment! He would spin around and around without realizing it was his own tail and he had total control over it! In fact, he should be mad at me! I got my amusement by watching him spin around. When you spin around and around in your life, who is getting entertainment value from it? I bet they're being productive in their lives!

When you expose yourself to people who are negative towards life and towards you, it may sink in. I did for a while. In high school, other kids made fun of me for wanting to work in Hollywood. Today, I work in Hollywood. Some of those kids have done well, but they aren't where they thought they would be. Some thought they would be athletes, or entrepreneurs. They are astonished that I stuck with it and made my path based on my dreams. Their lives are not any better or worse than mine, but they would have achieved more if they had paid less attention to criticising and making fun of others.

What did I learn from it? I learned that when I wonder if a woman is out with me because of what I do rather than who I am, or the kids in school took time out of their day to make fun of me, or all my ideas are bad; I know I'm doing something right. Turn your insecurity into something you can learn from and you will soon see that you have nothing to fear or be insecure about.

In times of adversity, think about sex

Actually, I don't know how thinking about sex can help, but at least it takes your mind off of your adversity for a few minutes. When I feel the whole world is against me and I want to cry or wave my white flag to surrender, I'm lucky to have a very competent team around me; you'll read about attracting the best people further on.

The one thing my team makes me do, is breathe! It's important; it makes the blood flow, calms emotions and allows for clear thinking. Once, I was fired by my distribution company. This was a bad thing because a publisher without distribution is like making a cake with the batter, but no oven; it goes nowhere. I knew I would be sued by all my authors, I would have no money coming in and my reputation would be completely destroyed.

A consultant had been brought on board a week earlier. He was calm and laughed. By then, he said, I had so many problems something good had to come of it. He set out to find distribution elsewhere. While he was doing that, I had a thought: "Why am I being a victim?" I had always wanted to create a major media conglomerate. I had thought it would happen later in life, but what was my excuse now? It was fear, cleverly hidden behind words like 'convenience', 'stress', 'feasibility', 'cost' and 'contacts'. The minute I evaluated it and saw it was fear, I created balance by evaluating the positives of entering into the situation and went forward!

Today, we have a distribution company arm, publishing arm and entertainment division arm. Was it magic? Not even close. I knew what I wanted to do. After the consultant saw my passion and determination, he went forward and found the right people. The avenues to achieving your dreams are the least of your problems—YOU are your worst problem! Overcome your fears and move forward.

Setting forth to sign the *Secret* authors didn't come without frustrations; it came with many! But my belief in myself was so strong and I was so passionate, that they had that excitement enter them and thereby signed with us!

It could all come crashing down tomorrow. Many times, it almost did. I wasn't afraid of that. I knew the world wouldn't end. Because of that, I was able to do what I did.

Synergy; what the hell does that mean?

Synergy is the perfect exchange in energy. When you want something that someone else can provide and they want something that you can provide; that's synergy. I love doing one-on-one sessions with people dealing with challenges. I love giving seminars as well, but with one-on-one sessions, you can see the difference in them after they leave the first session! As a Master Hypnotherapist, you would imagine I would be hypnotizing people more often than not, but it's actually the opposite. I speak to people first and often, I can see that their brain is working against them.

For instance, I had a 35-year old man come in who couldn't read. Imagine that; how incredibly frustrating! I asked him if he had gone to school. He had, up to Grade five. He said he had forgotten what he'd learned.

I knew better than that. I knew his brain had stored his ability to read, but wasn't presenting it to him out of fear. What was he afraid of, though? It turns out that this man had such low self-esteem he felt that he was worthless. He felt so low about himself that he actually cut off his ability to read and be on a par even with a Grade five student!

Ironically, he worked in a university. He wanted so badly to be part of a group of smart people, that without the ability to read, he put himself into a situation where reading is essential. I took him back to Grade five, unlocked the spelling basics and brought him back. Two weeks later, he had read my book, cover to cover.

I had another person who called me and told me that he had tried three times to kill himself. He asked to come and see me and I gladly invited him. After talking to him, he admitted he had never told his family about his suicide attempts. He had three psychiatrists and was on medication. He wanted to go to South America on a mountain climb for charity and maybe, he said, he would 'fall and kill himself, hopefully, or find serenity if he made it.' I looked at him, trying to be serious. But I ended up laughing; I couldn't help myself! I thought, 'here is someone who feels sorry for himself.' He felt that killing himself was necessary because he couldn't talk to anyone he felt would listen to him or care!

My girlfriend rarely listens to me when I criticize her shoe collection; but I've never thought of killing myself! I asked him if Darfur or North Korea had bigger problems than him. He said, 'yes.' I asked him if the New Orleans flood was bigger than his problem? He said, 'yes.' I said, "Have you spoken to your wife to know for sure if she cares or not?" He said, 'no.' So, the problems in the world dwarf his problem and his problem doesn't even exist since he's never taken the time or made the effort to resolve it!

I asked him if he was genuinely crazy. He said, 'no.' I asked him if he was smart; not even exceptionally smart, just average intelligence? He said, 'yes.' Then, to have three psychiatrists and need to go on a long hike to find peace from a life that isn't even chaotic; it seemed that he wanted attention, not to deal with a problem. This was proven by the fact that he wanted to book another session with me. When I gave him a bill for his first session, he never returned. I guess the problem was fixed.

I have seen so many people with a fear of money; myself included when I look in the mirror. The fear of money goes so deep and hides itself so well, it's very difficult to detect. Sometimes the fear is that rich people are evil or cheap. Sometimes it's that wealth can come with so many headaches. Others fear that money will expose the fact that they're not as good as they have made themselves out to be and will look foolish when others find out.

The rich love the headaches money can bring and will gladly deal with them. The poor think they are incapable of dealing with it. Can you guess which ones are the majority?

I know two women that have no fear of money. In a sense, I admire them. They can make money doing almost anything. One is a webmaster and the other is a manufacturer of various products. They're both strong woman, but they don't know that. So they act bold and brash and are loud and tough, just to prove it to themselves. But the fact is, they've both built million dollar businesses on their own. They ARE tough.

But I feel bad for them. They have no balance in their lives. They know how good they are professionally. But they're so afraid of their personal lives; they don't really have them, or at least healthy ones. That causes stress; it's work, no different than the stress created at their jobs.

One of them got cancer. The other has had one abusive relationship after another. Both are great woman; beautiful and loyal. But I wouldn't want to trade lives with either.

They are as afraid of having a healthy personal life as an average person is afraid of having a lot of money. Hard to believe, but it's true. You're thinking, "God, I'd love that! I have a personal life and there's nothing to it." Well, guess what? They say the same thing about people who can't seem to make any money.

Their fears of the past have put them into a vicious cycle that keeps them from leaving. When we put ourselves into our own vicious cycle, we get comfortable. We fear the unknown: The devil you know is better than the one you don't. It's almost like leaving would be worse; so we don't. Look at the woman in a bad relationship, the man with the terrible job, the woman who won't push herself at work because she believes it's futile.

Successful people see vicious cycles for what they are and *leave* them! They challenge themselves! I left a comfortable vicious cycle when I decided to take on the big boys by starting my own distribution company. When you leave, you find your true self. Either that, or bankruptcy court! Seriously! Look at the examples of Honda, and many others that I point out further into the book.

'I don't know what I want to do'

Yes you do. I have debated this for years with people and it only takes me five minutes to get to the center of the problem. Everyone, EVERYONE knows what they want to do in life. What stops them? It's fear, like everything else. I don't care what you say: You know.

There are only a few factors that suppress our desires: 1) The fear of breaking a moral or religious law. 2) Breaking our family's heart; or 3) Fear of failure and looking foolish.

We need to break this thinking up into comfortable pieces. What usually helps is when I say, "Let's remove reality and money necessities." That's when I get the truth. One person said, "I want to work with children." Another said, "I want to act." I even heard, "I want to do what you do." Do these sound unfathomable? I don't think so. Why the fear of admitting it? For the same reason I have been preaching to you in this book over and over again.

Fear is an illusion. It doesn't exist. Think of fear as fog. When you walk towards fog, you feel like you're going to run into something, or at least feel it as you enter. Then you stop and look around you and realize you've been in the fog all along and didn't even know or feel it! Why? Because it's just mist; compared to you, it's insubstantial. That's how fear works.

Money is the last thing to worry about. I don't care what business or career path you choose, there is money to be made. If you focus more on enjoying what you're doing, you'll see that money can be made. That's a promise that any successful person can make.

'Why do these things happen to me?'

With so many new theories coming out everyday, some bullshit, some not; I figured I might as well create one myself. All joking aside, if you look at yourself honestly, you'll see that it's true:

'The chaos you have inside is the chaos you have around you.'

Look at the people that cause you heartache, stress or anxiety. They're not there by coincidence or chance. They're there because you attracted them.

A Makeup Artist that I've worked with on a few productions was telling me a story about a person that she'd had to travel with and had only met on the day of the trip. They had a little pit stop and both went into a convenience store to buy some food. He rang up all of his purchases and then asked her to buy it for him because he didn't have the money. She was disgusted since he knowingly went into the store, brought the items to the cashier and had her ring it up, knowing he didn't have the money to pay for it.

I asked her what she had done to bring that to her. She looked at me, puzzled, since she said that they had been traveling together; who else was he going to ask? This is where you have to get specific with yourself. He had two choices to make: Either he could ask her because she is a sucker; or two, don't ask her because that would be a bad decision, for whatever reason.

He chose the first option; because the makeup artist is unsure of herself. Her unsure attitude causes a lost of stress and therefore, chaos. Because she is unsure of herself, she puts out a 'weak' energy rather than a 'strong' energy. This makes her easy pickings for someone who has no self-respect. This example reminds me of a television show in which former thieves were asked to evaluate random people on the street and report who they would pick as targets. There were no reasons for the people they chose; they just went on instinct. The producers later had a psychologist approach the people chosen by the criminals and interview them about their lives and history. Sure enough, every single target chosen by the thieves turned out to be a person who had low self-esteem. Some of them walked with their heads high and their shoulders straight, etc; but still the thieves picked them.

Going back to my makeup artist friend and her situation with the energy leech, could it have been avoided? The answer is yes. If her energy was strong enough and she was sure of herself, his energy would have been intimidated and he would have hesitated before acting in such a slimy way. This was later proven when she mentioned to me that she takes every job she's offered, for fear of losing an opportunity. I offered to her that you sometimes have to move down one notch to go up three. This scared her more than anything! All athletes will tell you that to 'up' their performance, they have to adjust their technique; which means taking a step back to get comfortable with the change. Then, you can go up two notches after doing so.

It's not about what you show on the outside; it's about what you *have* on the inside. If you evaluate the people who intimidate you; look at what they posses, how they act and why without words, they can discourage you from disrespecting them.

Dr. Bernstein, whom I mention again later in the book, has a very intimidating personality. I was so enamoured of that and wanted to know why. He carries himself with a strong core. He knows who he is, he is confident of his abilities and he knows what he's talking about. He does his research and he has the wisdom of experience; you really can't argue with him on a point since he'll back his point up with numerous sources. This creates an energy or aura that you don't want to mess with. Don't get me wrong; he still has insecurities like everyone else, but he doesn't have the same basic ones that most have since he has worked on them and defeated them.

Again, I will refer back to Dr. John Demartini. He has a great way of pointing out the balance in life. I use fog; he uses quantum physics.

Demartini will say that everything—yes, everything—that happens to you is something you have done to someone previously. It may not have been exactly the same; but it was done.

Johnny is a kid I've known since he was ten. He comes from a very troubled background. No father, a mother who lived in Greece and two half sisters who themselves have led vicious cycle lifestyles. Johnny just wanted to get through life in one piece. He thought if he could accomplish that, he would have done well for himself. When he was a grown man, he got in touch with me. He asked me for small tasks to do; which I gave him. He then started to model himself after what I did and how I acted. Soon he saw more possibilities for himself.

Playing the same game with me, I asked him what he wanted to do. He always said he didn't know. Finally, he admitted that it was photography. So I set him up with my friend, a photographer, who is very well known and in constant demand. The photographer had him doing small tasks here and there. Both the photographer and Johnny are very honest and loyal people. They both work hard and constantly like to learn; I knew they would be good together. Just by being around someone who is successful, you start to pick up on their habits and start to move yourself into a success stratosphere.

One day I got a call from Johnny. He was disappointed that he hadn't been paid by the photographer for his last job. It's really not any of my business, so I told him to send the photographer a polite reminder. The photographer again promised to do it, but with his schedule, he forgot. When he finally did send it, it was to the wrong address.

This is where it gets interesting. The photographer ironically called me the next day to tell me a client had booked him, but still hadn't paid him the deposit he had been promised several times. The photographer was irate that this person was taking up his time, but not committing. He asked me why this was happening. I told him that I'd gotten a call from Johnny who had told me the exact same story!

The photographer laughed and said, "but I'm not trying to screw him!" I responded with, "Neither is your client." So when you feel you are being treated unfairly, try to see objectively without ego or judgement, how did you do that to someone else? It will make you think about what your mother meant when she said, "what goes around, comes around." This will also make you think before you act.

Chapter 2:

Be Creative

How I sold my high school to Pepsi

It was an opportunity that I believed was right in front of me. It wasn't coming to me, so I had to go and get it. I created something from nothing.

I was sitting in the student association office, close to the school's front doors. A guy in a suit came in with an envelope. People dressed in suits didn't usually come to our high school. There were two ghettos in the neighbourhood and people sometimes got shot or stabbed on the property. I followed him into the office. He asked the secretary for the principal, who was in a meeting. The envelope the man was carrying had a Pepsi logo. When he put it in the mailbox for my principal, directly under my mailbox, it somehow fell into my mailbox, was taken to my office and opened.

After reading the letter, I phoned him and said, "My name is Sanjay Burman and I'm the president of the student association. My principal has authorized me to negotiate this deal." That's what ended up happening.

I was nervous about dealing with executives because they were sophisticated and worked for a major corporation; I was a high school student with an average of about fifty percent. What I kept in mind was that if I were straight to the point, I'd have very little room to say anything stupid. Whenever they talked to me, I'd forget the niceties and get to the point. I thought, *'Don't be rude or short with them; but get to the point. Tell them what you want. If they say they want to give you ten cents a can, don't go into a story about how you heard that another school got fifty cents per can. Just get to the point and say you're looking for twenty-five cents. That way, you can't hang yourself. There's too little space to do that.* That's the only thing I was worried about.

Using this approach, they took me seriously enough that the deal was fully negotiated and on the verge of final signing. They would own all the marketing rights, so they could put up posters and emblazon their logos on our textbooks. I wanted a Pizza Hut or something similar in the cafeteria and a significant stake in royalties on pop can sales. Plus, there was an adjoining elementary school with another 1500 students. I wanted a piece of that action as well. I thought that if those kids went through our high school and bought a Pepsi, that's a can sold on our property, so we should get a piece of that too. From there, it expanded into a plan that I could get this idea into other high schools and with one thing and another it grew into a $1.2-million deal.

After the deal died and I was suspended, another school board signed instead. It made newspaper headlines. I read the article and smiled because I knew it was the deal I had negotiated.

How I got started in movies

I didn't know what I was doing, just that there might be an opportunity to acquire content, deliver it to a studio or production company and get paid for it. It was a fast way of getting credit as a producer while doing less work. Nothing much was happening in my life. Private school, high school and film school had all kicked me out. My parents were saying goodbye to their dreams of my attending law school and goodbye to my future.

I started going to children's bookstores and getting to know the authors, who were usually listed in the phone book. It was that simple. Look in the phone book; I guarantee that one in three is listed. I went to the authors and said, "Look, I'm a kid and I'm learning the ropes. Give me the rights for six months and I guarantee I'll get something done with it." Sometimes it worked and sometimes it didn't. Generally it worked.

But I also found out how much other studios were bidding, because their agents or lawyers would call me, infuriated. They said I was circumventing them, not making offers the proper way. They said I was hurting their authors' careers because Paragon or Alliance might pay more. Then I'd go to Paragon or Alliance or whoever because I knew they were bidding on the project. I'd say, "Okay, these are the rights for the next six months." Because of the time limit, they had to put it into development quickly. I was getting credit from authors for getting their projects developed faster than anyone else.

People in the arts are generally considered bad business-people, because they usually aren't very interested in the business aspect of their world. Once I understood that, I found ways to fill that niche. As long as they knew that I was taking care of business for them, they'd start to trust me. As long as they continued to produce their creative work, it helped me. Sometimes I had to understand what other people were going through and comfort them in their insecurities. That way, I could position myself to move fast.

I Wanna Be Like Mike

When it comes to making introductions; I look for opportunities, win-win situations. That idea comes from Mike Ovitz. He worked the system to create a new system, one in which *he's* the power, rather than the clients or the studio. He was a super-agent who represented people from Tom Cruise down and he pretty much ran Hollywood. Then he thought, '*Why am I just representing directors, actors or writers when I could represent studios?*'

Ovitz sought Japanese corporations interested in buying studios. By controlling the financing, his agency became not only a one-stop shop for commercial production, music tours and actors or directors, but also a source for a line of credit for the production. Ovitz turned it around so that instead of being an agent who just got his clients jobs, he became the power base; gaining control from the clients or studios.

By doing everything out of the box and backwards, Ovitz established a whole new approach to production. A clear vision of the end-point enables you to see things other people haven't previously noticed. By going against the grain, you have a better shot at the best pickings, with less competition. Eventually, your competition will catch on, but by that point, you're already established.

Ovitz also taught that being in the centre spotlight makes you a target. If you search for quotes in the media by any agent at the Creative Artists Agency, you won't find much. They don't broadcast their deals, make comments to the press or show their faces. If nobody knows what you look like or how you speak, it's hard to find you. The less anyone knows about your business, the more you can manoeuvre. When you make a mistake, because everyone does; if you're in the spotlight, everybody sees it. If you're not in the spotlight, you can recover more quickly and move on. However to follow this, you need to have control over your ego. Very few do.

Because Ovitz was so good at putting people together, he became the networking king. I wanted to do the same thing. At first, I did it for everyone and everything, at every opportunity that presented itself. Then I realized there's more to take into account, like, what are the long-term benefits for both parties? How do these personalities mesh? Will one person become subservient to the other? I've learned not to force it. Now, I get people together for drinks or dinner and see if the conversation goes anywhere. I sit back and watch, evaluating the situation. If things work out; that's great. If I don't think it'll work; I leave it alone.

EXERCISE: Creativity

This is very simple. Decide on a book or magazine you'd like to have; then get your hands on it without paying for it. Don't steal it and remember you can only borrow from the library. Use your connections, any person or location you know, to obtain a copy. But you can't buy it with money and again, *don't steal it!* It's simple, but it will get you in the habit of being resourceful.

Chapter 3:

Step Up and Make It Happen

Finding Shoshanna Lonstein

I always go to the most influential people in the industry. With the Internet, it's easy to find out who and where they are. When I started, there wasn't much on the Internet yet, so I'd read newspapers. The people I talk to are always in the news. I might find out that so-and-so owns one company, but works through a small holding company. Research tells me who to look for.

This approach also applies to my love life. In the case of Shoshanna Lonstein, I had to do some research to find out where she hung out and with whom. I was able to parlay that into making phone calls.

I thought Shoshanna Lonstein was the most beautiful woman I'd ever seen. When I was in grade nine, she was dating Jerry Seinfeld. When I was just out of college, it was all over the papers that she'd broken up with him. I started reading about her in *Cosmo* and *People* and I saw that she was hanging out with fashion designers. I started to call people who knew her; top industry people. I couldn't just contact Shoshanna Lonstein directly. I called Donna Karan and Pamela Dennis and they both called me back. I said, "I'm head-over-heels in love with one of your friends. I'm the up-and-coming agent in Canada and I'd like to meet her." They laughed, but loved my confidence.

A week later, when I was in the boardroom with a client at the agency I worked for, the receptionist interrupted us to say there was a phone call for me. I said very politely, "No, I told you, no calls." She said, "I think you should take it." I said, "No, I'll take it later." Then she said, "It's Shoshanna. It's really her." I looked at my client and he said with a big smile, "You'd better take that call." I raced into my office, grabbed the phone and she said that people had been telling her I wanted to talk to her. I didn't know what they'd said, so I said the first thing that came to mind; that I had the greatest business proposition for her. All right, so I'm ballsier in business than I am in my personal life! This was on a Thursday. She said, "How about next Wednesday?" I said that would be no problem.

I told the owner of the agency that I needed to go to New York. He said, "I'm not paying for you to go to New York for a date." I had to think fast. There was no way I was going to miss this opportunity. I called a clothing company I'd done business with in high school and told them that if they flew me to New York, I'd give them the ultimate business proposition. They said okay. Shoshanna didn't know what the great business proposition was, the clothing company didn't know what the great business proposition was and incidentally, I didn't know what the great business proposition was, either! All I knew was that I was going to get a date with Shoshanna Lonstein.

I went to New York with the clothing company owner and head designer. We met with Shoshanna's father and the Vice President. The agents back home had made bets about whether she'd show up or just dismiss me as a stalker and not bother coming. I was getting nervous and feeling sick. I asked if I could use the washroom, and without waiting for their answer, I got up and left. Talk about freakish behaviour! It makes me shudder to think about now. I found the washroom, splashed water on my face and said to myself, "She's just a woman. Relax." Having pulled myself together, I started back toward the boardroom. Suddenly, she was right in front of me; I thought I'd pass out! We entered the boardroom together. I was quiet because I was sweating like a hog, meeting my future wife for the first time. I couldn't stop staring at her.

Looking back, I'm positive that Donna Karan and Pamela Dennis had told her, "This guy wants to ask you out." She was probably thinking, '*I want to see how long he's going to play this sham until he admits he was lying all this time.*' Everybody was looking at me wondering, '*why are we all here?*' Still, no one had asked me what this great business proposition was.

I took a deep breath and thought, '*Okay; it's do or die.*' I stood up. I *still* had no idea what the business proposition was going to be. I cleared my throat and said, "We're going to create the ultimate in athletic, formal clothing. It's going to be for the New York and LA businesswoman. She could walk to work, dressed for work and have the evening to herself without ever having to change. It'll be comfortable and athletic. It'll be designed by Shoshanna and made and manufactured by Bruzer."

Everyone was quiet. Then her father stood and said, "I love it!" I thought, '*I just made that up! All I want is a date with her!*' Shoshanna and her team left the boardroom. The designer and owner asked me how long I'd been working on the idea. I said for a long time.

Shoshanna came back by herself and she said, "It's a great idea. My father will talk specifics with you later. So, what are you doing now? If you're free, I can show you my studio."

'*Oh my God! She's asking me out!*' I thought. We walked out into the busy New York street and she linked her arm in mine. That's right, people!

We went back to Shoshanna's studio, where she had lingerie,

including a bustier, lined up. Under the hot lights, with me still sweating like a hog, she started holding up lingerie to herself and asking, "What do you think of this?" I reached up to undo my tie and somehow ripped the collar button off. I looked at it in my hand and I looked at her and thought, '*Oh my god, I look like an idiot.*' I turned and fled to the washroom again.

When we returned to the office, the clothing company guys were checking out fabrics. Shoshanna suggested we hook up for dinner. When I returned to the hotel with my team, we were all high-fiving each other. I was thinking, '*I've got my future wife.*' Later, she called to say she was running late and wouldn't be able to meet up with me after all. Unfortunately, that was the end of it.

At the agency, I won the bet. I had her father calling me every day asking about the weather and the deal and shopping for antiques. I thought he was setting us up for marriage.

Finally, one of the other agents said to me, "By the way, have you told her or her father that you're not Jewish? Burman's a Jewish name." I said, "I don't know what you mean." He said, "I have a request. Can I be at the wedding, please, when you tell them you're not Jewish?" I said, "I don't think it's a big deal." He left laughing.

During the next conversation with her dad I said, "Everybody thinks I'm Jewish because of my name and it's so funny because I'm not. Isn't that funny? Ha ha."

That was the last I heard from her or her father. Now she's married to a Jewish guy who looks like Jerry Seinfeld and they have a kid. Everything happens for a reason. I still don't know what the reason for that episode was, but I'm sure I'll figure it out someday.

Mark Breslin: I told him he was nuts and that it was almost criminal and fraudulent and I loved every minute of it. It makes you want to love the guy. To start a relationship from that distance, first of all and then to set up a business just to meet somebody. She didn't even get mad, from what I understand.

Tanya: I met Sanjay in '93 or '94. I was in the fashion industry, working for a sportswear company called Bruzer. My boss knew Sanjay, so he'd appear every now and then to meet with Jim. I think Jim was making T-shirts for Sanjay's high school. I knew him through work. Eventually, we went to New York. One of my bosses and I had a fabric show to go to and Sanjay had other business. We all drove down together. He tried to set us up with Shoshanna Lonstein. I don't know how he got the meeting, but he thought that Bruzer and Shoshanna would be a good fit. So he'd been calling her repeatedly and speaking with her dad and they finally agreed to a business meeting with us. I couldn't believe we were going into the meeting because I just didn't know what the goal was. I don't think anybody did. We were sitting in an Italian restaurant on Mulberry Street the night before the meeting, trying to figure out what to say and we never did. Then we went into the meeting; it was surreal. He was so nervous, he threw up beforehand. We met Shoshanna, her dad and her business partner. After the introduction, Sanjay politely excused himself and when he returned, I knew he'd been sick. Only Sanjay could've pulled that meeting off. It was unbelievable.

How to reach people with power and money

You're only six degrees away from anybody. The contact list I've cultivated now is so massive, that I always know who to go through to contact just about anybody. I have a friend whose father owns a big insurance brokerage firm that insures many high-wealth individuals. Sometimes, he can cut out five degrees of separation for me. But if I want to get to somebody he's never heard of, like the Sultan of Brunei, then I research to find out who does his banking or who his lawyer is in America. I contact that person and let him know why I want to get together with his client. Don't be afraid to be creative; I will keep saying that to you. The only thing stopping you is your own fear of rejection or failure.

How I met Shirley MacLaine

Shirley MacLaine was in town to shoot *Used People*. I was a big fan and I wanted to meet her. I knew she was into Hinduism, so I got a copy of the *Bhagavad-Gita*, took it to the set, convinced the staff that I was a film student and got someone to show me around the set. While I was touring, I was able to spot Shirley MacLaine's trailer. When my tour guide took me back to the front gate, I waited until she'd left and went back inside. I knocked on Shirley's trailer door. She was sitting there with her legs crossed, holding court with her entourage. Suddenly, it was like approaching a woman in a bar. I was really nervous; I was pretty young at the time, too.

"Miss MacLaine," I said, "I was sent here to give you a gift. May I speak with you privately?" She said okay, cleared everybody out and I walked in. "I would have thought you'd have more security," I commented. "Why, is that a bomb?" she asked.

I said 'no.' She opened the parcel, saw the book and said, "Oh, thank you." The way she said it, it must have been the eighteenth one she'd received that week.

I told her that I wanted to meet her because I wanted to be a movie director. She said, "Okay, what have you done?" I admitted that I hadn't done anything. She rephrased the question, "What have you directed?" I said I hadn't directed anything yet. "Okay, you want to work in Hollywood, you come to me, but you haven't done a thing. You haven't worked, you haven't produced a film, you haven't directed a film and you haven't starred in a film. By your age, I'd already done how many things? Why would you come to me?"

Feeling chagrined, I put my hands in my pockets and looked down. She actually said to me, "Take your hands out of your pockets and look at me when I'm talking to you." Suddenly, it was like I was listening to my grandmother. I felt scared. I took my hands out of my pockets and she said, "Do you understand what I'm saying?" I said, "Yes, ma'am."

Then she eased up. "I'll tell you what. The Stephen Spielbergs and Tom Cruises are all waiting for you to make your big entry into Hollywood. Start doing your homework and working at it and in no time you'll be there. Now go." Then she sent me packing. I swear that's exactly what happened! I got lectured by Shirley MacLaine. She made me realize that I was behind and that I'd better start working harder.

I don't know if she does that to everybody, and I don't know if anybody else would get that same opportunity. I saw it and grabbed it. The truth is, when I left, I felt disappointed; like I hadn't gotten anything out of it. It wasn't until a few weeks later that I fully realized what she was saying to me: get into fifth gear and start moving! Saying that you're young and just want to have fun, doesn't apply to creating success. If you're young and work hard, you'll have the rest of your life to have fun. Bill Gates doesn't answer to anybody when he's on vacation because when he was young he worked. Now he can enjoy the rest of his life. That was the first event that snapped me into fifth gear.

How Ken Thompson helped me with a school project

When I was still in school, I had to write an English essay on a Canadian personality. I picked Canada's richest man, Ken Thompson. He actually called me one night to help me with my essay. I couldn't write fast enough to keep up with what he was saying, so finally he started dictating my essay to me. The irony is that I got a C on that paper. I couldn't believe it and neither could he.

"It's my story, it's my life," he said. "How did you get a C on it? Did you write what I told you?" I said, "Yeah, I wrote down everything and she said that it wasn't explicit enough." "But it's my life!" he said. "How could it not be explicit enough?"

I've always felt that the best way to succeed is to go the person directly or go to a person directly related to what you want to become. I've always sought out the best people to apprentice with and learn from.

Ajay Burman: I got a call one night at nine o'clock. The guy on the other end of the line was coughing and could barely talk. He asked for Sanjay, who'd already gone to bed. He goes to bed early and he gets up early. I told the caller he had gone to bed, but I'd let him know who's calling. He said, "This is Ken Thompson." I almost dropped the phone. Sanjay has that charisma that gets people to look at him twice.

More American than Americans

Instinct will tell me who is or isn't the right person; which is or isn't the right script. I used to think it was a fluke, but now I know it's instinct. When I was a kid, I took every script and ran with it because I thought it could be a winner. Today, I can pick and choose. Even if something I've turned down wins an Oscar, there was a reason I didn't want it. I'm okay with putting it back and not having my name attached to it.

Bruce Rosenberg: The Hollywood guys really like him, but he's an anomaly in Canada. Canadians don't like him. He's more Hollywood than the Hollywood guys, more American than the Americans. He's aggressive. Unless you're a salesperson ingrained with the cold call instinct, it's hard to make contact with somebody. Most people will sound like idiots. But he finds a way.

What people mean when they say I'm "more American than Americans" is that I'm focused on the bigger picture. An example is that if James Cameron had pitched the movie *Titanic* to a Canadian studio, they would've said, "Holy God, that's $120-million. We can't do it." Even if you could show them the future in which the movie wins all those Oscars, they'd still tell you it's too expensive. When Cameron took *Titanic* to an American studio, they said, "What a great movie. We're going to clean up on this one. Let's find a way to pay for it." Fox and Paramount studios teamed up to make *Titanic*, a rarity in this competitive industry. The point is that they understood it was going to be a great thing and they could figure out the costs later.

In Canada, we tend to look at the hurdles first. Canadians perceive sitting in front of Cronenberg's house as virtually stalking the man. Americans almost want to ask, "Why didn't you just break into his house and put it on his desk? Are you lazy or something, just sitting in your car?" More on that story later.

I was born and raised in Canada. This is my home; I don't want anyone thinking that I'm biting the hand that's fed me. However, if you're an overachiever, Canada can be frustrating. We're a passive country. To be honest, I like it that way. We play nice with the world. But in Canada, don't think people will jump to accommodate you because you have gold in your hands. A perfect example is that in spite of all the small successes I've achieved and the executives I have relationships with, they still make me sign release forms before pitching them something. For Canadians, the first thought is to protect one's self, rather than to see what's being offered. A US network has never asked me for anything except a winning idea.

Debbie Nightingale: He wasn't afraid of anyone or anything. That allowed him to travel in circles that other people would have been intimidated by. You have to be careful that you're not too arrogant, but when you talk about stuff enough, people start to believe that you can deliver what you say you can deliver. I think that his willingness to be aggressive, some degree of arrogance, assuming that he can talk to certain people, stood him in good stead. I always liked him personally. When he did the big talk, about the people he met or made deals with, I enjoyed it. I was charmed by it. Others might be offended.

Steve Nyman: He really understands the concept of networking and that's what makes him successful. When you know people and you're open to new ideas, you're always trying to create a business opportunity of some sort. He's very good at it.

EXERCISE: Networking

Pick someone you admire. It doesn't have to be a major celebrity; it might be someone in your community. Research this person, going beyond a simple Google check. Push to find out personal information like their hobbies, habits and quirks. Once you have that data, evaluate why you admire them. Based on your newfound knowledge, look within your immediate circle of people to find out who can help you meet this person. Remember, there might be a few degrees of separation. Again, be creative! No idea is crazy, so try it. If you run into a dead-end, try another path. Make sure it's legal!

Chapter 4:

Don't Take "No"

How I convinced three of the richest executives in Canada to finance my college film project

In film school, I thought I'd come 'home,' but quickly realized that I hadn't. To me, film school seemed like a place where rebellious lesbians made avant-garde films; which didn't interest me. It was a tumultuous year; I didn't want to be there. I was living in the basement apartment of a townhouse and it was suffocating because it had no windows. The couple who owned the townhouse were nice enough, but they kept to themselves. Every night my classmates went back to the city and I was the only one left in a small town that shut down at nine every evening.

One day, I said to my teacher, "I don't have enough money to make a final-year film. How do I get sponsorship?" She told me no one had ever received financing or sponsorship. "Why should you, when you're only a first-year student?" she asked. When she said it that way, it sounded like a challenge. Now I *had* to get sponsorship.

I found the newspaper listing of the year's sixty highest paid executives. I went down the list, calling them all. Through trial and error, I discovered that the ones who made $10-million or more had voicemail. The ones who made $1- to $5-million had no voicemail and the ones who made $600,000 to $1-million had voicemail. Don't ask me why. The newspaper gave the person's name, income and company name, so finding their phone numbers wasn't a problem. In all my calls, I was very sincere in saying, "I need help; I'm in school and I'm having a hard time. I want to make this film. Please help me start my career."

I tried calling after regular business hours. If they had an automated attendant, it went right to their voicemail. If not, it went to their personal assistant. When I phoned Conrad Black, I got to his voicemail the first time and his assistant the second. It was the same with Seaton McLean.

With Placer Dome Canada President, John Willson, I got his voicemail three times. After my second message, I got a call back from someone in accounting who said, "He's sending you a cheque. It takes two weeks to process." I called the accountant back and said, "I appreciate your help, but I can't wait two weeks." The accounting person called back to say he was FedExing the cheque. My third call to Willson, after I'd finished principal photography, was to say, "thank you very much." None of these three people wanted any sort of film credit and they didn't want me to talk about how they'd assisted me. (Sorry guys, but your generosity can't be ignored! Too bad everyone wasn't like you.)

The exercise of making all these calls was a great experience. Of the sixty people I'd called, only three called back. It was a lot of phone calls to make for only three responses, but it was worth it. It also showed me what I wanted to become once I was successful. I wanted to be one of those three who calls back. I mean, how much money do you really need? How many yachts can you have before you're finally able to turn around and say, "This kid might end up being the next Gates or Spielberg. I'm going to toss him some money; $500 or $1000." I'm still talking about it because I'll never forget it. I was in dire straits and I really needed help. It's beside the point that they could just write it off. What stood out was that they did it for me, when they'd never met me and knew nothing about me.

That being said, Conrad Black's assistant told me, "There's a cheque waiting for you. I don't know what you said to him, but he doesn't usually do this kind of thing." When I went to pick up the cheque, I found his office was an old bank building. When I walked in, I thought I was in an art gallery. There were huge paintings everywhere. There were paintings up the stairway and in the office and it was all very plush. I got a cashier's cheque with Black's name on it. I photocopied it because I knew nobody would believe me otherwise. That's how I financed the film.

At Alliance Atlantis, Seaton McLean never met with me again. His assistant said, "Here's your editor, here's your post-production coordinator and here's all the film you'll need." He opened a refrigerator and the shelves were stacked with really expensive film stock. I'd been planning on using cheap, low-grade film, but they gave me the expensive, professional film stock they used. I got the film made and while watching it, realized I was the worst director on the face of the earth. Reality is a great friend to have; he's always there for you when you least want him around.

How I met Norman Jewison

Another example of constant calling was with Dina Lieberman, an executive for Toronto Women in Film and Television. I called her because my parents' printing company was producing her newsletters. I must have called her twenty times a day, at home and at work, asking her questions about the industry. She finally said, "You've got to stop calling me because of my husband, my kids and my dinner. I've got other priorities. I'm going to get you a job because that's the only way you'll ever leave me alone." I was only fourteen.

She found a job for me with Debbie Nightingale, who at the time was active with the Toronto International Film Festival. She'd bring in speakers, big-name directors and producers to speak at symposiums. Debbie thrived on my questions. She could handle my asking her a million questions. Plus, she ran that division at TIFF and had other staff working for her. She allowed me to be rebellious. Dina's attitude was more like that of my parents; "You've got to do your homework." But Debbie would write notes excusing me from class.

I kept telling Debbie that I had to meet Norman Jewison. She took me to the opening party for *Black Robe*. It was in a Cirque de Soleil tent, there was a chocolate fountain and limos everywhere; it blew my mind. I was going around asking everyone, "Do you know Norman Jewison?" I didn't even know what he looked like, so I walked up to everyone, asking if they knew him. Everyone's response was, "He was just here." I was determined to meet him. In fact, while working for Debbie, I'd run my errands early just so I could sit in front of his office to eat lunch. I finally got my shot at meeting him at another TIFF function later that year. After doing the rounds again, asking everyone if they'd seen him, I walked up to a gentleman with a baseball cap and beard and asked, "Have you seen Norman Jewison around?" He replied, "I'm Norman Jewison." Having finally met him, I didn't know what to say. I ended up saying nothing. He looked at me like I was weird and walked way. Thus ended my first meeting with Norman Jewison.

Debbie Nightingale: A fourteen-year-old kid with that kind of initiative impressed me right off the bat. He used to wear a suit to work; even if he hadn't, that's still how I'd picture him because he had that kind of seriousness. He had a very specific goal for getting the job at the trade forum with me and that was to meet Norman Jewison. He said that if he met Norman, he'd conquer the world. He worked very hard for us that summer, doing laborious, boring jobs. The film centre had just started doing their barbeques at the end of the festival. He wanted to get to the barbeque and we arranged for it. After that, he was on his own. Afterward, I spoke with him and I asked if he had met Norman. He told me the story of how he had met a distinguished-looking gentleman and asked him, "I'd appreciate it if you could help me. The only thing I've ever wanted to do in my life is meet Norman Jewison, because I want to be in the film business. Can you help me?" And he responded, "I am Norman Jewison." He got what he wanted, by being focused on what he wanted.

When you get "no"

I think persistence is part of my gene pool. It's worse when it's your personal life, when there's a woman you really want; you keep calling her and eventually she calls the cops. You don't see her as a person anymore. She's just a goal. But persistence is the greatest thing for succeeding in your professional life, because a deal can't walk, a deal can't think, and a deal has no feelings.

I moderate my persistence when I'm dealing with creative personalities, because my hardcore persistent personality rubs them the wrong way. But people like Conrad Black and Phil Kent get off on persistence. They're not threatened by it. I'd call Phil three times a day and he loved it. You can't get to that position without having that kind of persistence yourself, so it reminds them of themselves. Not many people have it. Yes, sometimes it's upsetting to others, but if your persistence is modified from person to person, most people will take a liking to it and to you.

However, just being persistent isn't enough. You have to deliver the goods, too. If you're constantly asking for raises at work, great, but you need to show you're worth it. Your value has to be apparent through increased productivity, increased quality and working well with others. If I had repeatedly called all the influential people in my life without showing them that I was working very hard and attaining my goals, I wouldn't have received the same level of support from them.

Dr. Bernstein, a well-known diet doctor with a chain of clinics throughout North America, told me to stop kissing ass; it's obvious and people don't respect it. People like Spielberg don't care about you. If you're in trouble, it doesn't concern them. The only person who can help you is yourself. If you don't help yourself, who will? That really resonated with me; especially since he said it to me at my birthday party! I have to be persistent. Subconsciously, I call or e-mail certain people, because of the habit of repetition. With some people in my life, if I don't call them every day, they call me that evening. They miss me.

Persistence comes from within

Persistence comes from within. It's an inner need. You can't stop thinking about it, whatever it is, even for a second, because you want it so badly. Yes, obsession is another word for it. With healthy obsession comes Albert Einstein, Soichiro Honda, Colonel Sanders and many others. You never doubt yourself, never think you're wrong. Sometimes people don't understand what they should or shouldn't do, when it's simple: You've got to follow your heart and visualize from your heart, the perfect picture of accomplishing your dreams. First you feel the desire and persistence is simply an external manifestation of that. If your intense desire is to act, keep acting and eventually you'll hit the ball out of the park. Many actors have done just that. They pack up and move to LA with nothing but their intentions. They go from audition to audition and eventually they just hit one out of the park. The constant desire to achieve will eventually be positively actualized; just remember to be careful what you wish for, because it will happen, but maybe not the way you imagined it!

> *Sonia:* It's important to question the intention behind why you're being persistent. I'll use physical exercise as an analogy. If you push and push and don't take a break, you could injure yourself and never reach your goals. Whereas if you trust the ebbs and flows of the process and know when to slow down or take a break and when to modify the goals, you're persistent but also flexible.

You won't win all the time—but that's okay

The one person I couldn't break down through persistence was Jodie Foster's publicist. I was still only fourteen, but I tried everything. I followed him everywhere, bombarding him with questions. This guy wouldn't budge. He had no interest in me, wanted nothing to do with me, and almost swore at me: "Get lost! I'm busy." He had no warmth inside him whatsoever. He was just mean.

Persistence doesn't always work. Sometimes you'll piss people off. But I'd rather piss one person off and get four people on my side using this approach. Besides, it's not personal. Do I care if you don't like me because I'm persistent? It's better to find out now than later. I might as well know up front. I will not let anyone stand in the way of me achieving my goals. If that's not you, re-evaluate why you're allowing yourself to be held back.

I believe that I'm not perfect and I haven't yet achieved what I want to do. I can say it will work for you because, so far, it's worked for me. One strong belief I have is that if you continuously go for it, no matter how many times you strike out, eventually you'll hit one out of the park. Persistence, persistence, persistence. That's the one thing that has worked for every successful person.

How Colonel Sanders and Soichiro Honda succeeded

Colonel Sanders was in his sixties, and felt his pension income was too small, so he went to numerous restaurants, trying to sell his chicken recipe. They all refused him. Most people couldn't imagine going to so many different restaurants, being that persistent in the face of such rejection. But if he could do it at his age and eventually succeed; you can do it at any age.

Often what people call 'bad ideas' are new ideas and their negative reaction may be caused by fear of their own failure. They're in a rut. If you're talking to somebody who's not an entrepreneur, they won't always recognize a great idea. That's okay! That's their right and their comfort zone. Don't let it stop you! If you hit a mountain, do you just stop and go home? No; you go around it!

Soichiro Honda's story underlines the value of a great new idea. During the war, his factory was destroyed three times, but he still had spare parts lying around, so he attached them to his bike to create the first moped. When people saw it, they wanted their own mopeds. That's how Honda started. Although he hoped to some day build cars to compete against Toyota, he started by building something unique, created by his persistence to achieve.

Often, the things we think are big and significant, like fear of rejection or failure, really aren't that daunting. It's all a matter of perspective. My father used to get angry at me for stupid things, like wearing my shoes in the house. I finally said, "Dad, if you meet God, do you want to say you had a heart attack because your son wore shoes in the house?" It made him think for a moment. Sure, he'd get angry again, but it worked briefly anyway.

Mark Breslin: Sanjay has no phone fear. That's very rare. When I have to make a cold call, like most people, I wince and beat around the bush and go for a walk, whatever I can to defer it. Sanjay will leap in and think nothing of calling the most important person in the business and badgering the secretary until he finally gets to them. That's an amazing skill. It's the skill of a great salesman or entrepreneur and I give him full credit for that. A lot of other people do that as well. Not everybody has the stomach for that kind of rejection, but he's able to do it, again and again. He's impervious to rejection, which is a great trait. Maybe not in life, but in business. He does not withdraw.

EXERCISE: Persistence

You don't have to start by asking Conrad Black for money. Try asking people in your social circle for sponsorship for a marathon or a donation for a charity event. You'll be doing something you can feel good about, but you're also getting in the habit of asking. It's what Jack Canfield calls "The Aladdin Factor": Ask and you have a fifty percent chance of receiving. Don't ask and you have a one hundred percent change of not receiving.

If the person you ask for sponsorship says no, try to find a new angle, a new way of asking, to get them to say yes. Don't be a pain, don't be overly aggressive and don't get upset if they say no; it's not personal. Don't ever show them your disappointment. Generally, people don't enjoy upsetting or disappointing others and may avoid you in future if they know they have. Keep a poker face, smile and ask: "May I ask why you don't want to?" If they say they've already made donations to other charities, convince them that the charity you're working for is well established, it's a good cause and although you don't normally do this kind of thing, this particular charity has captured your heart. If you asked for $20, they might come in with $10 or $5, but at least you've persuaded them to participate.

Chapter 5:

Earn Respect, Don't Expect Respect

Most influential people I know could have made a phone call or used a personal favour to start my career. In some cases I was fortunate, but ninety-five percent of the time, they didn't. They answered my questions, gave me advice and introduced me to people. If I didn't do it on my own, get the project off the ground, they wouldn't respect me and I wouldn't respect myself. A rich kid who gets a car from his parents doesn't appreciate it; a kid who has to work and saves to buy her own car appreciates it and takes care of it. Sure, sometimes it's upsetting or frustrating but at the end of the day you feel proud because you've done it yourself.

I think the whole 'have fun because you're young' thing is a crock. Bill Gates worked hard when he was young; he had little fun, but he has a great life now. The same applies to Michael Dell. I've always believed that because I'm young, I have a lot of energy and I can outwork my competition. I also believe there's a discipline involved. Kids whose parents give them everything have no idea how to survive. I've dated women like that. They might have had great business minds, but they don't care because they can get whatever they want without effort. If you have the discipline to say no to those free handouts and work hard for things, you'll come out much stronger and better able to take care of yourself. Don't look at what you're missing; those who have it might not really be in a better position. Appreciate what you do have and use it to your best advantage.

It's unfortunate, but I've noticed that my generation has less and less integrity. This could be because we're getting lazier in life; this is indicated by statistics of higher than ever divorce rates and bankruptcies. We give up on our dreams so easily today.

I frown on the idea of 'image' later in the book. I think people who are worried about their image take less risks and miss out on opportunities due to fear. But I might contradict that statement when I say worry about your integrity. Life for you will revolve around your integrity. It's what will get people to invest in you, fear you, love and help you. Integrity can't be bought, can't be taken and can't be threatened, unless you make it so.

I remember Kris Gilbert, a very talented production manager and one of my many mentors, told me that integrity is what you have when you can't afford to buy people's trust. It's true! You know from your own experience. Think about the favour you did for someone you know is a constant liar. The only reason you did it was for a direct payback. But think about someone you're inspired by, who conducts himself with true integrity. You do that person a favour even when there is no direct payback or even without a payback at all! The reason is because you feel inspired to be a better person around them.

Now why does the second person in the above example make you feel inspired around them? The trick that most people lack; whether it be in philosophy, religion, integrity, honesty and ethics is that they practice what they preach, even when it's INconvenient. That's it. It sounds simple; but it's extremely hard. People quote free speech when they want to voice an opinion, but forget about free speech when they have to listen to someone who opposes their beliefs.

Integrity and honesty have to be practiced every day, every minute. A friend of mine listens to philosophical audio books all the time. He lives by and breathes by them, until it becomes inconvenient. We were going to be travelling together for a mutual business appointment. The person he needed to see was not confirming and he didn't want to go until that happened. I had booked my ticket, but my travel agent booked the wrong date by mistake. My friend freaked out at my travel agent! He flipped like it was his ticket that was wrong when he hadn't even booked his yet! It was my ticket and my problem that my agent quickly rectified. I saw a side of my friend that made me lose a little respect for him since he preached what he needed to learn. He had built his existence on the knowledge of philosophy, but when it most needed to be practiced, he lost it!

We spoke about it a month later and I told him that he needed to practice what he preached, not what he needed to learn. He replied with, "That's hard." Of course it is! Everyone would do it, otherwise! You may not like me, you may not agree with me, but the one thing I know is that for most people in my life, I have their respect. Because of that, I make sure to live my life in a way that maintains that respect. Life can be easy or it can be hard. To make life easy, be selfish, don't have integrity and just stumble through it. It will be unexciting and a waste of your time, but it will be easy. Or, take the hard route, suffer, sweat, bleed and in the end, you will have experienced greatness! Greatness is what is remembered long after you are dead. Give something back to the world that will outlive you. It doesn't have to be Microsoft, even if it's just your reputation. By the way, even Microsoft is not the greatness that Gates wants to leave the world with; it's his charity. What's your greatness? Show it with integrity.

Don't be desperate!

Desperation is lying, cheating or deceiving to get what you want. I've used peoples' names to get into places and I've been caught once or twice. It's embarrassing because you lose credibility with both sides. I did that when I was younger because I wanted to get into somebody's office. I only do unethical things when I'm desperate. Desperation causes you to lose yourself, behave uncharacteristically. After *Spider*, I created a show on CBC's Newsworld, but I was living an empty life.

Kevin Sullivan, the producer of *Road To Avonlea*, once said to me, "Every person will have a second chance at something great if they wait it out." I interpret that as, *don't be desperate!* My desperation has messed things up for me a few times. I've had to learn to respect myself and have faith that the right thing will come along.

For example, the best-known children's series I represented was the *Tom and Liz Austin Mysteries*, by Eric Wilson. Each book took place in a different province, highlighting that province's scenery. If Tom and Liz solved a mystery in Vancouver, the scene would be set with mountains and water; in Edmonton, it was the West Edmonton Mall. One of the first books I ever read was *Murder on the Canadian*. Who knew that one day I'd be trying to get the rights to it?

Eric Wilson was a bit difficult to deal with, but he let me do what I needed to do. In retrospect, when he said he'd never sign a contract with me, I should have ceased, but I didn't because I was hungry for the deal. Sure enough, when I got a production company aboard, they had problems with Mr. Wilson as well. I had to massage the deal and finally they came to an agreement. When the production company turned to me, since I'd brokered the deal but didn't have a signed contract, all they offered me was an internship on the set. It was insulting! To add insult to injury and really cement my lesson in desperation, the only lawyer who'd represent me on the deal in exchange for commission convinced me that the production company was actually being very fair. Don't be desperate. Something else will come along. If not, complain to Kevin Sullivan, not me!

I'll give you another story about desperation that shows my idiotic way of handling things. My car gets me around. I have a virtual office; my phone, laptop and cell phone travel with me everywhere. At one point, things were so bad, I couldn't afford car insurance. So I drove without it, illegally, for a few months.

Around the fifth month, I slid into the car in front of me. I panicked, since without insurance, I'd be responsible for paying any damages out of my own pocket. When the woman got out of her car, I noticed a cross hanging from her rear-view mirror. I thought to myself, *'I'd better start talking fast.'* She inspected her car and saw there was just a minor dent on the fender. She wasn't worried about it and was willing to drop the matter. I breathed a sigh of relief. Then her sister emerged from the car and said, "There could be internal damage. Get his insurance."

I was desperately looking for a stall, while pulling out my wallet to give them my non-existent insurance information. "I see you're on your way to church," I blurted out. It was a Sunday morning, so it seemed like a good bet. Then I said that God really had it in for me. The driver looked sympathetic and asked me why I thought that. I told her I'd had so much bad luck lately. She took pity on me and I was able to negotiate a deal with her. I'd see that her car was fixed and to avoid her having to rent a car while it was in the garage, I'd drive her to work and then home again for as long as was necessary.

Do you know what it's like to hit somebody's car and then become their taxi service? She'd call and say, "I have to go to work early today." This was my lesson from God. To top it off, she'd recite the bible in the car. I always said God had a sense of humour and I bet he was laughing hard at that one. It was the most awkward twenty minutes every morning and every evening. It got to the point that her co-workers got to know who I was and would even say hi to me. She didn't insist on insurance, but I renewed mine immediately and will never let it lapse again. You might get away with doing something desperate for five months, but sooner or later, you'll get nailed.

Embellish, Just Don't Lie

It's never easy to get to influential people. There's a trick to doing it. When I was younger, I was caught lying a few times. Finally, somebody pulled me aside and said that because I was young, I could get away with it, but that if I kept on lying and getting caught, people would stop believing me. It's like crying wolf; if you do it too often, people will stop accepting your calls. If you want to embellish—and people assume you're embellishing anyway—make sure there's some truth behind it.

Remember though, leaders can sniff out when you're being deceitful and people, in general, aren't stupid. They know whether you're being sincere. People will respect you, trust you and be there for you if you're sincere. Being sincere has to do with being honest. Don't just tell people what they want to hear; tell them what they *need* to hear. Then they'll know you're being honest.

People say that about me: I say exactly what's on my mind. Sometimes I don't want to say something because I don't want to hurt them. But if I don't tell people what they need to hear, they won't know. Being honest with them gives them an opportunity to see the faults and correct them.

Embellishment is okay because there's still truth and if you don't embellish, you're the worst salesperson in the world. You should be passionate as hell. No matter what you're selling, ultimately you're selling yourself.

I started to network with people who knew influential people. If I was trying to get to Bill and I knew Joe and Joe knew Bill, then I'd go to Joe and say, "Don't you think it'd be a good idea if I talked to Bill about this?" If he said yes, I'd call Bill and say, "Joe said it would be a good idea if I called you." Technically it's embellished, but it's still truthful. When he calls Joe, the conversation won't be dead-on accurate. It'll be, "Do you know Sanjay?" "Yes, I know him. He's doing his best and trying hard. He was talking about you the other day." So Bill assumes Joe has sent me to him for a reason. Then he calls me back. Most people don't even do the research; they assume that if Joe sent you, then you've got something worthwhile to talk about. But never take that chance; I've done that and been caught looking foolish a few times.

When there's no time to waste, go directly to the top. Sherry Lansing was the chairperson of Paramount Pictures when I started managing actors. I called her and said that I needed a certain actor, one of my clients, to audition for one of her films. She said that as Chairperson of the studio, she didn't set up auditions. I said, "I know. That's why I'm calling you. Please." She did actually set up an audition for one of my clients, which is unheard of in Hollywood. She has a reputation for being very nice, but she was especially nice to me. No, my client didn't get the part, but Cameron Crowe saw her audition and that was worth gold.

If at First You Don't Succeed, You're Running About Average

My entire formal education, from private school to college, was a problem that had to be turned to my advantage. Teachers are now more aware of kids who can't sit still and learn from a book. That was me. I learned from the teachers with whom I bonded and would sit down with me after class. I learned a lot more after hours than during the school day. Every problem you endure, you can learn from. Sometimes you might feel bitter about it, but overcome that to learn something from it. Today, I can read people faster, listen better, take more interest in other people and I'm actually fascinated by the learning process. In school, when I was being forced to learn, it wasn't fun. Hypnotherapy is a great example of something I've learned as an adult.

How I lost the bid for *Alias Grace*

After I read Margaret Atwood's *Alias Grace*, my vision for the film version starred Rene Zellweger and would be directed by Jodie Foster. The jail that Atwood had written about was being torn down. I thought it'd be great to shoot in that facility, so the government would put a hold on its demolition. I knew there were three studios bidding on this project. I thought, the thicker the book, the more money.

I said to Atwood's agent, "I'll give her $500,000 US ten days from the date she signs." Of course, I had no money. Her agent was very nice to me, but he could tell I was inexperienced and showed me how to rewrite the option agreement. His words were, "It's obvious you don't know what you're doing, since everyone else has bid about $400,000 less than you have. If we go forward with your proposal and you can't pay it, you'll be in trouble. Get some other agreements and come back to me."

I sent the book to Jodie Foster's assistant, revealing the option agreement, how much I'd bid. You might be thinking, '*What an idiot. He just gave away his cards.*' But I needed Jodie Foster on board.

I retrospect I should've played it halfway. I should have said I had an option agreement and that they should attach themselves if they're interested. The other studios were bidding $100-200,000. I spoke to the president of Paragon Entertainment, John Slan and he said, "You're bidding how much? We were bidding $160,000. You've got yourself a bit of problem because this is a rich deal and she's going to sign it and you're going to get sued." He looked at me to see if I was scared, but the only response I could honestly give was—and I wasn't being a show-off—"Wouldn't *Variety* make us the headline story the next day?" It didn't bother me because once she found out I was a kid, there was no way the lawsuit would go a second round. I just wanted the front page of *Variety* shouting that Jodie Foster was suing me.

It was in the *Toronto Star* a week later that Jodie Foster had signed *Alias Grace* for $750,000. I thought to myself, "*Isn't it convenient that she bid $250,000 over us?*" They'd read the information I'd sent and turned it to their advantage. I was so disappointed. When I found out that Jodie wanted to star in it, I knew the chemistry was wrong. Sure enough, it still hasn't been made. It just shows that opportunities come and go. The ones that go aren't meant to be. That was the first deal on which I got really badly stung. I've learned to have more of a poker face and not expose all my cards.

EXERCISE: Challenges

Continuing on your path after meeting adversity is something you have to experience and motivate yourself to do on your own. Every day, challenge yourself to do something you hate. It won't kill you. Well, hopefully. Don't try jumping off a building without a parachute. But if you're shy with strangers, try starting a conversation with someone new, perhaps with the next person you see in a public place. If you're afraid of asking for a raise, ask for the raise anyway. Do something that scares you every day for the next five days. Any kind of fear points to something that you need to work on to overcome.

Chapter 6:

Don't Burn Bridges, Unless It Can't Be Helped

How I got *Spider* made

After leaving Characters, I started an agency called Burman Management Group that was then bought by a venture capitalist. For a while, we shared an office and he taught me the fundamentals of money: How bankers and investors work, how money flows. I got a financial education that only Harvard MBAs get. I applied this knowledge to management. You control the industry by understanding how money works.

Mace Neufeld, who produced *Hunt for Red October*, *General's Daughter* and *Patriot Games*, also produced a film called *Bless the Child* with Kim Basinger. I advised an up-and-coming producer and client of mine to take the job as executive assistant to Mace Neufeld. I told him that he'd learn a lot and also have unbelievable contacts by the end of it. If Mace Neufeld wanted anything, a drink of water or an east-facing room, his assistant would deal with it.

He was working for Mace Neufeld, but he was also my client, so I said to him, "Say my name once a day. I don't care how or when; just keep saying it once a day." By the thirtieth day, Mace was asking, "Who's Sanjay?" My client told him, "Sanjay's an up-and-coming agent, someone you should meet with."

So Mace came in to find this twenty-three-year-old kid in a venture capitalist's office. He couldn't quite put it together, but he knew it was going to be an interesting meeting. Ten minutes into my spiel, he decided that I was going to be his agent.

Mace FedExed me a script; it was a very dark piece set in England. By calling friends at independent studios, I learned they'd all seen it before. They advised me to let it die. Mike Nash, Vice-President of Paramount Classics, gave me the following advice: "If you take this on, it's going to look like you're out of the loop, since everyone has read it." He and I became good friends from that meeting and he taught me a lot. But I couldn't return to Mace and say I couldn't do it. I had to be very creative to find a way to get it done. I circulated it to some other directors, but I knew their ideas were different from Mace's.

Then, director David Cronenberg was suggested to me by the same client who was working for Mace. He said, "It's a weird script. Why not try David Cronenberg?" I knew I wouldn't get to Cronenberg through his agency, so I thought, *We live in the same city, so why not visit him?* We found out where he lives, so we sat in our little Toyota outside this place with Lamborghinis and Porsches going by. It must have looked like we were staking out his house. Finally, Cronenberg walked by. I jumped out of the car and said, "Oh my God, what a coincidence! Ralph Fiennes wants to do this movie, but he says he'll only do it if you direct." To which Cronenberg replied, "Okay, if that's true, send me a letter." I got back in the car thinking, *I don't know Ralph Fiennes, and I don't even know if he likes the script. What am I going to do now?*

I called Fiennes and told his people that David Cronenberg wanted to do the movie, but would only do it if Ralph took the lead role. Fiennes read it and loved it. The producer who actually owned the script was a woman in England. I had an agreement with her about my fee. Cronenberg and Fiennes met and they agreed to do it. But of course I hadn't told them that I'd manipulated the situation. I was so scared. I kept thinking I was going to get a phone call any minute saying, "You lied. We're walking."

This was an opportunity; I could have said that I couldn't take the script anywhere, that nobody would take the script. But I wanted it to be made because it would increase my success. I was prepared to create a situation in which people could call me a liar. But the gods were smiling. Cronenberg and Fiennes agreed to do it and the movie was made.

Unfortunately, I didn't have a written agreement and Cronenberg and I got into a dispute. The lawyers got involved and settled for half of what I was owed. It was enough that I could buy a new car, rent my own office and pay my lawyer. I had been warned not to fall in love with the illusion—the boardroom, the venture capitalist's office—if it wasn't supporting me anymore. I'd gotten to the point where I was working from home; I didn't want to go into the office anymore. It was seed money to start again.

Another lesson I learned from this is that even when there is an agreement in place, when someone wants to screw you, they still can. How do you win? You don't, but sometimes getting screwed is good for you. You survive it and it makes you less scared the next time around. *It's going to happen sometime,* so just do your job the best you can. If you do a great job and 'they' screw you, they lose because you won't work with them again. If they treat you fairly, then you'll be even more loyal and hard working.

Don't be afraid of litigation

I had a tumultuous relationship with the venture capitalist. Our expectations were completely different and that resulted in him suing me.

It's important not to be afraid of being sued. Somebody once told me, you're only as big as the people who sue you. It wasn't a joke. It's true. I sue and I'm sued. I was sued by my venture capitalist partner because he felt I was at fault for not turning a profit. I tried to explain that developing a property takes years, but he couldn't understand that. To him, it was a betrayal. I had a good team on my side, my lawyer. He fought back on my behalf and won. I learned from that scenario and now I can predict the possibility in other people. I don't care how much money is on the line; if I don't think we have a compatible relationship, I say no.

The Cronenberg film almost came to a lawsuit because I felt I'd been betrayed both professionally and personally. But the minute the project was completed, my animosity toward him evaporated. It's not personal. I'd say hi if I met any of these people on the street. I invited Cronenberg to my birthday party; I'm proud of that.

Some of my clients are petrified of being sued because they can't fathom losing half-a-million dollars. No matter how much you lose, it won't kill you. It's part of the adventure of life. Sometimes bills can't be paid. That won't kill you either. No matter what happens, it's not as bad as you think.

And if you're one of those people who sit in judgement saying, "He gets sued because he puts himself in those situations," you're right! I'm the king of my own domain! If you think your favourite celebrity, musician, businessperson or politician doesn't have lawsuits, you're mistaken. If you want to lead, be prepared to face the consequences as well as the glory.

How personal relationships impact your success

For years, I'd had an up-and-down relationship with this woman. I found out on Christmas Day that she'd married another man. It was a tough time. I questioned myself, my life, my integrity, and why I'd liked her in the first place. When I analyzed the situation, I realized there was a side of me that was drawn into this negative scenario, that wanted to help her, solve her problems. Sometimes it's challenging to understand why we choose the people we do, but we have to.

This brings me to something else I've learned: Choose positive people. It's one reason I urge you to connect with the top people you admire. Being around the energy of success and accomplishment will put you in the same mindset.

Mark Breslin: He was screwed on that deal [Spider], but people in the film business screw each other all the time in precisely this way. Sanjay doggedly refused to take it. He won. That speaks well of Sanjay's stick-to-it-iveness. They say that people who make it in business are those who will not let go. They're like a dog with a bone. He took on people who were way more powerful than he was and he badgered them into giving him what he deserved.

It's impossible not to burn bridges

I have a different take on reputation than most people. With corporate people, reputation is everything. Between promotions and jobs, reputation runs their life. For me, because I'm an entrepreneur, I don't depend on anybody for my job. The reputation I want is that of a risk-taker and loose cannon. You can choose to work with me or not; that's your prerogative.

In fact, I think having a pristine reputation can be detrimental, because you're so worried about safeguarding it that you might not take risks or say what needs to be said. Some of my business partners are very concerned about their reputations. With these people, when a little success happens, they want to fit in and don't want their reputations tarnished. I think everybody should have the reputation for being dependable. Otherwise I don't have much faith in reputation as a virtue. I think it's a bit of a hindrance.

Leave the past in the past - or at least out run it!

Now, as you may have figured out, my love life sucks. Yes, it's the balance that I'm trying to learn and master; however, I can't really go out on dates while writing this book for YOU, can I? That being said, this happens to be a lesson that not only have I had to learn numerous times, but three people around me have faced it, just this past week. Therefore I thought I should include this in the book and maybe give you your money's worth.

It's great to reminisce about the past. I do it; likely you and everyone else does it, as well. The worst part is getting nostalgic on the subway or bus and smiling about that funny joke, or scenario that took place and realizing everyone around you is staring at you because you're smiling like an idiot. To me, thinking about the past is a great way to see how far you have come in life, but can also lead to the negative emotion of wishing you could relive it.

This applies to both your professional and personal life. We all think about the promotion we passed up, the girlfriend or boyfriend we had deep feelings for, or perhaps, being trapped in your house with a friend or family member through a storm; where the two of you bonded and had a lot of fun that day. It's natural and actually produces endorphins to make you feel good.

The only problem is that sometimes these people, opportunities or scenarios come back and give us the chance to relive them; or so we think! I have had many occasions where my past came back, but not to relive the 'good days'; to haunt me. The girl that I fell in love with first, the job that I passed up that came with a very nice salary and old friends I hadn't seen since high school. It's easy to want to go 'back' there; your memory of it was great!

There's only one problem.

You're not the same person you were back then. That is the ONLY problem. It's not about them, it's not about the times, it's not about the economy; it's about you. It is best to leave the past in the past. If you look back at a certain situation that didn't work out, you would see that it happened for the best. I kept hoping, obsessing and working towards success at the age of 17. If it had happened, I would have been very screwed up today. I wasn't ready for it and even though it seemed like it was just my bad luck or bad judgement to not take some of the offers that were given to me, I would have to say it happened for the best, looking back.

I've recently had that situation with a girl I was madly in love with; my first love, actually. I met her just after her break up with a boyfriend. I was there for her, her shoulder to cry on and eventually…the dreaded best friend. Yeesh.

Fourteen years later, we were living on the same street! We

met up six months after trading emails back and forth but iron-ically, never ran into each other on the street. Anyway, she came over to my place one evening and we talked. Turns out she was living with a guy and it wasn't working out. Yup, I tried to pick up where things left off and by being a friend (and no more), she left her boyfriend. Turns out she was married, divorced, lived with this guy, had suffered a miscarriage and was still as scared and insecure; living in a fantasy Disneyworld and seeing it through rose-coloured glasses. Me, in my infinite wisdom, tried to date her again. She was also interested, since my life had taken a much different path.

Before we could really start dating, I saw her for what she was and not the fantasy I had created and ended it. Now, she wasn't better or worse than me, but she was different, with different goals and I knew she couldn't work well in my lifestyle of constant growth.

The same thing happened to me when I flew down to New York for a breakfast meeting with Ari Emmanuelle, best known as the inspiration for the crazy agent **Ari** on **Entourage**. At the time of our meeting I had no money, no luck and no choice but to go where life took me. Ari was great. He was very success-ful with a huge client list like Ben Affleck, Matt Damon, Mark Wahlberg and others. He was interested in having me work in his agency, **Endeavour.** I said I would think about it and later decided that it wasn't the route for me. I told him that I wanted to produce and be my own boss. He respected that and figured out very quickly that I had no money, so he asked the waiter to 'pack my lunch' and put it on his tab.

Phil Kent, Chairman of Turner Broadcasting had set up that meeting for me. Hearing good things from Ari, he called me and asked what I wanted to do. When I told him my deci-sion, he agreed fully, stating, "You're not a Phil Kent, you're a

Ted Turner and will eventually have Phil Kent's working for you." Best thing he ever said to me, other than 'You're an idiot,' when I told him I wanted to marry Jennifer Love Hewitt.

Some years later, the struggle had increased and opportunities in my eyes were dwindling (which today I realize wasn't true, I just chose to see it that way), I called Ari and asked him if that offer was still open. He not only said no, but the way he said it was almost like he lost respect for me. He wanted me to succeed as leader of my own ship and all of a sudden, I wanted to go back to him; it could only be out of desperation.

A great contact in the entertainment industry, great memories of a girl I once knew, all screwed thanks to me trying to go back.

If you don't get the lesson in the story, I suggest you read the quote by Phil Kent above.

Let it Go!

If I gave you a bowl of water and asked you to carry it around the block without spilling a drop, you would most likely carry it with both hands and stare directly at it to watch the water's balance and avoid spillage. The problem with that is, yes, you would bring it back without a drop spilled, but you would also miss the birds, the flowers, the kids playing or all the beautiful things around you that may never be repeated!

When we look at our future, we often stare exactly at what we think is important, but many times isn't! The first thing that comes to most people's mind is money. 'I need money to pay my bills, I need money to pay for vacations, clothes, etc.' Yes, you do need it, but staring directly at it will bring less of it, since you will have missed out on the elements or opportunities that present themselves to you on your peripheral horizon.

When I was 26, I had a deal with Showtime for a movie that was being developed from a book my client had authored. We had negotiated the deal and agreed upon the cast, director and schedule. I was understandably excited since I had pleased my client, built a relationship with the president of Showtime and it was going to be a good movie. The contract was sent to me via FedEx. When it got to me, I got a call three hours later from legal affairs, saying I shouldn't sign it; word from Viacom was that they were cutting their budget and movie slate in half and mine was in the cut pile. The contract was in my hand! It was worth about $50,000 to me. I don't know if I had tears in my eyes, but it sure felt like it.

Back then, I never evaluated my life the way I understand it to be now, so I just focused on the fact that I lost the deal. I felt disappointed for two weeks and didn't bother to push anything else for a while. More recently, my engineer for our audio books, Ashton, called me to tell me he had a new contract to do some work for another company. He got the first job and even got paid in full before the job was done! They sent him another cheque for another job. The day he was going to the bank, they called him and asked him not to cash it since they had cancelled the job and the cheque as well.

As disappointed as he was, he stayed balanced and decided that it would come back around to him when the time was right. As he said that to himself, he opened another envelope only to find a payment for another job he had done. Unlike myself, Ashton kept his eye on his surroundings and not on the bowl of water. Did some get spilled? Yes. Was it worth it? Absolutely.

This isn't complicated. You have to adjust your thinking, since depression, disappointment and pain are just the fantasies that come from creating expectations that aren't met. If

Ashton had relied on that payment, spent it in his head and started to think about future payments from that company, he would have been distraught by them cancelling the job. Instead, he took it in stride and focused more on the fact that he got the first payment, so he was actually ahead and since he never started the second job, it was nothing lost and nothing gained. Then, he was able to see beyond the little box and find another cheque!

So go ahead, spill some water! It will be worth it and you will see that almost immediately.

Chapter 7:

Fewer "Yes" Men

'Yes' Men will screw you at the most inopportune times. They're more like ass-kissers. They'll agree to everything and the minute you turn around, they'll stab you in the back. Why do people keep them? Simple: they're great for our egos. To be told every decision is right, to be praised for our high intelligence (I *know* they're lying to me then) and to be made to feel special, makes us fall under their spell and want them around. Don't be fooled! Keep people around you who will tell you the truth, even when it isn't pretty or what you want to hear. You don't need to go looking for these people, because they'll be attracted to you at the right time.

When the high-school fiasco happened, I was expelled. It was a long enough suspension that I wouldn't have been able to graduate. My father thought I should apologize, but I thought the school couldn't justify punishing me, so I called a lawyer for the first time in my life. I told him my situation and said I'd pay him a buck. He laughed pretty hard, but he still helped me out. Eventually he was made a Supreme Court judge. After he helped me, it was the end of that. I never heard from him again nor was I able to contact him. He was like an angel. Conrad Black was there when I needed him, when I was desperate. Those are the people you learn from. You can't just take their actions for granted. Everybody has had at least one of those people come into their lives, but they may not realize or appreciate it. I'm always looking for them and I'm always thankful for them.

Successful people have experienced adversity to get where they are. They can guide and motivate you when you're ready to give up. Everybody needs someone to pick them up off their heels. Hanging out with successful people is both enlightening and motivational. They tell great stories. You start to feel like you belong to their elite group and that allows you to see how they've succeeded. I hang out with Vice Presidents of corporations, CEOs and entrepreneurs. Being around them helps generate new ideas, but it also makes you feel like you're getting somewhere. It's easy to meet those people; they're everywhere you go, at parties, at the gym. Since I don't usually go to parties, I arrange meetings just by cold calling. I read about them and ten minutes later I'm calling their office. It's a magical connection. I send out the message that I need their help and guidance and that I appreciate their wisdom. For every ten successful people I meet, maybe five invite me into their lives to learn.

How I met Mark Breslin

A perfect example of establishing contact with someone influential is how I met Mark Breslin. He was buying a hotdog from a street vendor at the time. Mark owns the world's biggest chain of comedy clubs, called Yuk Yuk's. Jim Carrey and others have gotten their start at his clubs. I saw him at the hotdog stand, went up to him and asked if he was Mark Breslin. When I extended my hand, he recoiled and asked, "What are you selling?" That threw me off, since it was a rejection on some level, but I said I just wanted to learn about how he did business. After that, he was very warm. What bonded us on that first meeting was that I confessed that I only had one suit, no money and I didn't know what to do with my life. In spite of his power and success, Mark never talked down to me; he talked to me as an equal. He said that I only needed one suit to get in any door. It was true. I actually had to borrow a dollar from him to get back on the subway. I've always been able to confide in him. He's extremely loyal to me. He stands by me both publicly and privately.

Mark Breslin: Sanjay claims and I have no reason to doubt him, that I've know him since he was fourteen or fifteen years old because he shadowed me one day. He called me up and said he wanted to be in the business. I don't remember it, but my memory's not particularly great and there's too much stuff in there. I don't remember this event, but he says it's true and I believe him. He said I was nice to him. He used to show up a lot at different events I'd do and try to hang off the vibe and see if there was a business opportunity. He became one of those people in my life—and there are a number of them—who I developed an informal mentor relationship with and I tried to introduce him to people. It got busy with him around the time he started working for Characters. I helped him get that job by putting in a good word for him. That's when we started to talk a lot, see each other a lot and started exchanging information. Then he left Characters and we talked about him getting involved in our agency, but we didn't want to do that. We'd talk about potential clients that we liked or didn't like. He introduced his clients to me so I could see if they were any good. Sometimes they were and sometimes they weren't. On top of that, he put one specific deal together for us, which was this book deal. From what I can tell, he did a good job with it. I think Sanjay's more interested in the deal than the product, whereas I'm more interested in the product than the deal. My partner's a marketing guy, so he's like Sanjay.

There's nobody more grateful or attentive than Sanjay. There's nothing worse than the curse of the consultant, when you give advice and the person ignores it. But Sanjay rarely ignores my advice.

The team that backs you is your life support system. They can make you fly or die. Pick carefully. The best way to keep the best is not necessarily by paying them the most, but by giving them the most respect. I try to keep everyone's bigger individual goals in mind and help them attain those as they help me with mine. My team was built over many years and started with Bruce.

How I met my *Consigliore,* Bruce Rosenberg

Initially, I had another lawyer from Bruce's firm. But I'd see Bruce and we'd talk about music or whatever, while I was still going to meetings with my lawyer. But I never felt quite comfortable around my lawyer; I didn't trust his abilities or his faith in me. One day, I called up Bruce instead and we've been together ever since.

At the beginning, I said, "I have nothing and I'm paying you nothing, but I believe in my dream. This is where I want to be. When I achieve it, your personal dreams will be achieved as well." The team came together and we began our journey.

Bruce Rosenberg came to me at a time when I was at my lowest. Bruce motivated me almost daily, even though I told him at least 500 times that I couldn't continue in the movie industry, that the fight just didn't get any easier. Almost every morning, for a year, I'd call him and tell him I was quitting. Bruce never asked for anything in return. He was very loyal and has taught me a lot about human dynamics.

Bruce isn't a typical lawyer who went to a big law firm straight out of school; he was taught how to be street smart by a street-smart lawyer. He knows how to find people's weak spots and he goes for the jugular. He taught me about negotiations, human nature, how to read signs. He can calculate an individual's personality based on a letter. Bruce's advice was, 'walk in prepared to lose the deal.' That way, you're not emotionally attached to winning it. It's so true. If it happens, it happens. If it doesn't, it doesn't. He doesn't care. He doesn't allow himself to care. He keeps reality in check for me.

Everyone should have someone like Bruce in their lives. He's like an angel who allows me to do what I need to and removes the hurdles for me to accomplish my goals. *Every* successful person has someone like Bruce, someone who doesn't like the spotlight and is happy being the person behind the person. They whisper in your ear and calculate the odds for you. Don't worry; your Bruce will find you. Stay focused on your big goal and when you need them, they'll come into your life.

My companies have great teams

Catherine, my book editor, keeps everything organized and the creative process happy. Talent can be sensitive, fragile and emotionally unstable. They don't necessarily communicate well because they're living in a box with their computer for six months; they need comforting. They need somebody to tell them that they're moving forward and that their work is great. I'm not the person for that, but Catherine will make any writer comfortable; even if they've never written a word before.

Javad, my cover designer, is creative, quick and accommodating. As long as you don't cross him, he'll bend over backwards for you.

An almost obsessive-compulsive perfectionist, Malcolm does layout and interior design. If something is out of whack, he'll spend all night fixing it, if necessary.

My distributors, very careful, conservative people, like to keep things in order. They want to participate in the design and presentation of the books. They also happen to be one of the largest in North America. Why did they bet on BurmanBooks, the smallest publisher in their stable? Because they believe in us.

As long as we're reliable and keep aiming higher, we'll maintain the same team. Look around. Will your support system help you succeed or bump you off? Most of the time, I don't know what the end result will be, because I don't have to! I fully trust my team. They cover me and make me look good.

> *Sydnee:* Sanjay matched me up with the perfect co-author. Then he didn't get involved in what my book was about, except for the title and that allowed Luke and me to create a really fantastic book. I don't even know if he's read the book! He knows it doesn't matter, because he knows the material is good and this allows him to set up distribution and work great deals. Once the book is out there with the right publicity, the content will continue to sell itself. So he does what he knows best and that is concentrate on putting the deals together.

On the film front, I have Brendan, who's very level-headed. I tend to attract very level-headed, calm people; maybe because that's what I need around me. If you have more than one Sanjay on a team, you'll have problems. Trust me on this; sometimes I want to fire myself for getting on my own nerves! I also have agents, lawyers and managers who trust and believe in me.

Maybe I haven't made a $100-million movie, but I've impressed them.

The minute you know you need something in your life, once you identify it, admit you have that need and the right person will appear. Unexpectedly, you'll be introduced to that person. That's how it comes together. I don't go searching; if you give it a chance, it'll work. But for it to work, you have to change your core beliefs and really want to achieve your dreams, bring them into reality; don't keep them as dreams. Your team has no time for dreamers.

People flow into and through my life

It's like talking to a beautiful woman in a club. You can talk to her without an agenda and she'll love it, but once you start thinking about how to ask her out, she'll sense that energy and her defences will engage. It's the same with any other type of human interaction. Don't talk to people because you want to get something out of them. Talk to them because you find them interesting. Kevin Wright, Head of Programming for The Family Channel, gave me some great advice before my first trip to LA. He said go and speak to people without a script or agenda. It worked, because they didn't feel any desperation. They were happy to give me advice, more advice than they would have if I'd tried to get something from them.

Vanessa: If you go to a party, just go and enjoy the wine or the dessert. If you meet somebody, you meet them. If you have that positive and happy energy around you, people in the business will come to you. If you keep it a mystery, what you do, people will ask.

Gestalt therapy espouses the idea that you bring people into your life and allow them to be who they are. If they prove to be incompatible with your beliefs, eventually they'll flow through your system. The people you like, you keep. That works.

I trust everybody, believe they're sincere and believe they're good, unless I'm proven wrong. Generally, I don't write or sign contracts. I may do so to appease my lawyers and insurance company, but a handshake agreement is all I need. If someone betrays me, I simply don't do business with them again. That's their loss, not mine. If they prove loyal, then I know we'll be working together forever and I'll make sure that they also profit from the relationship. It's hard to trust once you've been stung, but you have to. Trust everyone. Life's easier when you do. If you encounter someone you immediately don't trust, listen to that instinct and be guided by it. But otherwise, trust is paramount to success.

In my business, marketing is important, so I know a lot of journalists. Journalists spend the majority of their time researching to find a special angle on their story or on a person. As I suggested earlier, whoever you want to get close to, research them, get to know them, learn what makes them tick, what their passions are. If you're in a room with David Geffen, talk art. If you're in a room with Bill Gates, talk bridge. If you're in a room with an actor, talk about them. I've found that the best places to meet people are those I don't want to go. If I'd prefer to go home for a quiet evening, instead I'll make myself have a shower, get dressed and go out. The minute I don't want to go somewhere, the times I've force myself to go, I've always met somebody who can help me or teach me something.

EXERCISE: Bonding with a mentor

Anyone can be a mentor. Perhaps one of your neighbours or co-workers has achieved success or done something you respect them for. Ask them for advice around a business, creative or personal matter. Tell them you'd value their input on a certain situation. A mentor is somebody who will spend time with you, talk to you, give you the benefit of their experience and invest some of their energy in you. That's it. It doesn't have to be Donald Trump.

Chapter 8:

Shut Up! And Be Truthful to Yourself

N ever say, "I know." Phil Kent said this, as did my dad. The minute you say, "I know," you're blocking out further information. I had a client who used to say, "I know, I know," and I wanted to teach him a lesson. When he said "I know," I created a situation that was the complete opposite of what he'd expected. When he came back and asked what had happened, I responded, "You said you knew." He never said, "I know" after that.

My father used to say, "Every time you say 'I know,' you shut people up." Now, it's become habitual for me to listen until whoever I'm talking to runs out of things to say. Always hear somebody out. You might get that one piece of information you need, the piece that seals the deal or alters your thinking.

You don't need to tell people that you know. That's just your ego talking. Let go of the idea that if you don't know, people will think you're stupid. As Phil says, "you have two ears and one mouth for a reason. Listen more than you speak."

The same thing goes for your internal voice. If you can stop your ego from saying, "I know," and listen to and respect the voice that's deep inside you, the one that's truly you, you'll be able to create a happier and more fulfilled life for yourself. You've got to be real, to be yourself. Trying to be me or anybody else, involves putting on a mask and you'll lose confidence in yourself and credibility with others. Begin by being yourself. Whether somebody likes you or doesn't like you, it's better to know right away, before you've invested much time or energy in the relationship.

Everybody who's successful has been honest with themselves. It's hard to sleep at night when you're pretending to be someone you're not. You make excuses to justify your position. You start internalizing your emotions. Eventually, your body rebels against you and you start to become physically ill. Some people turn to drugs or alcohol, two strong signs of internal unhappiness; self-medicating deadens feelings for a while. A lot of corporate CEOs are in rough shape.

I don't think there's a day I get up and don't wish I had a job that gave me a regular salary. But there's a magnetic pull that says no. Something clicks with me. I keep wondering if I'm going in the wrong direction. I'll make one more phone call and if it doesn't work out, I try it another angle before giving up. Then I do that another fifty times.

It has to be internal, something that comes from within, something that gets you out of bed. It's the difference between being a leader and being a follower. Ten percent of the population are leaders and ninety percent are followers. The ten percent endure more adversity than the ninety percent ever will, but nature pulls them toward it. Some people are afraid of that and avoid leadership roles so they don't have to experience it. Others rise to the top, but don't have what it takes to be leaders and end up being very unhappy people.

The perfect analogy is the story of the general and the prisoner. The general says to the prisoner, "Tomorrow morning you're facing the firing squad, but you have a choice. You can face the firing squad or walk through that door." The prisoner asks, "What's behind the door?" The general answers, "Nobody knows, because nobody has ever chosen it." The next morning, the prisoner chooses to go before the firing squad and is executed. The general's secretary asks, "What's behind the door?" The general answers, "Freedom, but nobody ever takes it, because it's unknown." I repeat that story to myself every time I make an excuse and talk myself out of something. It's just fear of the unknown.

How to persist in the face of adversity

When we're emotional, we're very self-centred. When a deal dies, or when you're constantly struggling, it can feel like the end of the world. Everyone experiences this sometimes. When you're in it, remember that other people have been through it and survived. You will too, if you just keep your eye on the ball.

You may not think you're moving forward, because you've experienced continuous defeats. For two years solid, I was defeated again and again, but all the while I was learning what not to do. It might sound mundane, but you really do begin to see the warning signs when the same things happen repeatedly. By becoming aware of them, you can stop yourself before getting into trouble again. Adversity is something that has to be fought internally, as well as externally. Internally, you're in a constant state of emotional trauma; you want to give up. When it's extreme, internal adversity can lead to nervous breakdown or even suicide. When you're unable to express it, it feels like you're alone.

What is success?

To me, success is achieving the credibility to become a motivational speaker who's free to do that 150 days a year. Many people don't seem to realize that success doesn't necessarily mean having money or fame, but achieving happiness. Sure, it's a cliché. But I guarantee you that Britney Spears or Madonna wake up in the morning thinking, "God, who's going to pressure me today?" or worrying about the photographers swarming their houses.

> *Jennifer (hypnotherapy client):* It's about life choices. You make those choices. We all have to take responsibility for the choices we make. It's too easy to blame somebody else. You don't need anybody else to make you happy; you don't need to depend on anybody else. Your world's not going to fall apart if you're by yourself. That's very important. Other individuals are great and enhance your life, but your life won't fall apart without them. I don't need to look to external factors or other people for validation. I can get validation from within. When I know who I am, I'm not as easily influenced by other people.

Some people thrive on money, others on personal satisfaction. Money doesn't give you as much power as people think and personal satisfaction won't buy you a Porsche. Determine what success means to you. Some people do dishonest things for money or things that are out of character. Money simply allows you to gain the material possessions you want. Personal satisfaction gives you power and meaningful personal relationships. Gandhi had nothing; he died almost penniless, but was one of the most powerful, influential people in the world at the time.

If you do things in a realistic style that's honest to who you are, you'll be more comfortable with yourself and better able to sleep at night. It's the same emotion as the adversity of being kicked down and then getting up again because you know there's something better.

When I left Characters, it was scary; depression set in immediately. I didn't want to get out of bed, I went to bars at night with friends and stayed out too late. Strangely, my father never said anything. He understood I was going through a period of depression and he let me ride it out. Sometimes I wanted to quit the industry, but something always made me get up and my mentors and angels kept me going.

No matter what your age is, if you want to leave your job for a dream, do it! The worst that can happen is you may have to get another job. It won't kill you and you'll learn some things about yourself. You'll be actively living your life; fully engaged with it. That's not easy to do. It's a journey with lots of rough patches. But I guarantee you'll be a lot happier with yourself, because you'll truly understand what's important to you.

Fear of leaving a career or job is normal and makes you think about the next step. But don't let the fear become an excuse. Taking that next step will make your life better, both internally and externally. Stay and although nobody will judge you, you will have limited your potential success and sacrificed true happiness by staying safe. It's like eating cabbage every day for the rest of your life and justifying it by saying that if you switch to steak instead, bad things might happen. There are numerous examples of corporate executives quitting their high-paying, high-stress jobs to become chefs or something considered menial and less powerful, simply because it gives them life fulfilment.

To deal with fear, I ask myself, "What am I afraid of?" I narrow down my answer, analyzing it until it's very specific so I can determine what I'm *actually* afraid of. If I keep narrowing it down, eventually I'll find it doesn't exist. Fear is usually something we create, a thought process designed to protect ourselves from the unknown. Nelson Mandela said, "Our deepest fear is not that we are inadequate, our deepest fear is that we are powerful beyond measure." People fear success, not failure. Our fears are based on our illusions.

Ron Joyce, who co-owned Tim Horton's, sets a great example. He was a cop. I know a lot of police officers; they're not entrepreneurs, they follow orders. For Joyce to leave police work because he wasn't happy doing it and start a coffee and doughnut shop instead, was a huge risk, one that probably caused him many sleepless nights. But he invested some money, co-founding the operation with hockey player Tim Horton and today he's sitting on $700-million and free to sail around the world on his yacht. You have to take risks to afford luxuries.

I must emphasize that it's not an easy trek. I've learned a lot about myself through adversity along the way. Adversity has made me 100 times stronger and 100 times smarter and much more creative than I was.

I always thought I was dumb, uncreative and insignificant. I may not be as smart as the next guy, but I have the right people around me to make sure that what needs to get done, gets done. I can't calculate company earnings or manuscript word counts, but I have people to do that for me. I'm not stupid, but I'm not as smart as Catherine is as an editor, or Luke is as a writer. But I'm creative, because I have an innate ability to bring those people together.

Adversity has also taught me about compassion by showing me what I *don't* want to become. I've dated trust-fund women who were so cheap, they wouldn't help others, even though it was in their power to do so. Often, the richer you get, the stingier you get. I don't know why that is, but I've seen it many times. Most people reading this will say that they wouldn't be that way if they were rich. But I suspect those stingy rich people said that too. Money comes and money goes; just ask Donald Trump. I've had it and I've lost it. I'll have it again and I'll lose it again. Ultimately, I want to have fun and ensure that the people I know and work with are enjoying the ride too.

> *Krista:* In high school, Sanjay had a vision that he talked about a lot and he never strayed from his vision. It was his dream to be a director or producer. People laughed at him in high school because he talked so much about it and it was so far from the reality of where he was at that time. But he was very consistent with his vision. He made it happen.

EXERCISE: Getting what you really want

Begin by writing down something you desire. It might be meeting someone, a state of being or a material possession. Be very specific; if you want a car, write down all the details, the make, model, colour, everything. Next, visualize yourself in the situation; talking to that person, feeling calm or driving that car. Really put yourself there and make it as real as possible. Get emotionally involved. That emotional energy will send your thoughts out into the universe where it can connect with others. Done daily, this can be a very powerful and fulfilling visualization.

Chapter 9:

Opportunities Knock

Sometimes I've had an opportunity come without preparing for it, like producing a movie. I didn't have the experience, but I grabbed the opportunity anyway and the right people came to me to make it a reality. People and opportunities are both energy. If you put out positive energy, you'll get positive opportunities and positive people will enter your life. That doesn't necessarily mean they'll be perfect or that they won't trip you up in some way, but at least they'll help take the project to the next level. That's what happens when you find the right opportunity or when it finds you.

> *Ajay Burman:* Sanjay approached a writer for a deal and he said, "You're only seventeen years old. How can you represent me?" Sanjay said, "Is it the age you're interested in or the bottom line you're interested in? If it's the age, why don't you find somebody who's seventy-nine? Maybe he's the best person for you, if that's what you're after. But if you want your books turned into movies, I'm the guy for you." He came to see Sanjay at the house one day and said to me, "This boy, at this age, has given me an inspiration I've never had before."

If an opportunity comes up more than once, it's worth investigating. It's supposed to be in your life. If you miss it and if it's meant to be there, it'll come around again. It's like the old joke about the man who's trapped on the roof of his house during

a flood. A boat comes by and the man says, "God will save me."
Then a yacht comes by and he says, "God will save me." Then
a helicopter flies over and he repeats, "God will save me." He
drowns and goes to Heaven. When he asks God, "Why didn't
you save me?" God replies, "I sent two boats and a helicopter.
What more did you want?" If an opportunity knocks three
times, take it!

> *Sonia:* What Sanjay does with hypnosis is something
> that a lot of therapies don't do. He's all about taking
> responsibility for yourself and looking at your part in
> all relationships. It's very empowering. He doesn't say,
> "You're a victim." Instead, he asks, "What did you do to
> attract this?" or "What selfish motive did you have?" It's
> very empowering and it's an important tool for change,
> because the only thing you can change is yourself.
>
> Sanjay believes that everything is in his control and that
> if he's persistent enough, he can turn a pig into a king.
> Ultimately, you can't. It's like being the eternal optimist
> and there's nothing wrong with that, but you can't change
> certain people unless they want to change themselves.

Swimming Upstream

The publishing company is an example of swimming
upstream. I've made the authors partners, not only on gross
sales, but on expenses too. Consequently, we can mount better
launches and promote the books more heavily. Some people
think it's insane; some of the authors even said that after they'd
signed on the dotted line.

The way I package movies, the way I packaged *Spider*, is
different from the way people usually do it. Teach yourself to

automatically think outside the box. All the studios told me *Spider* was dead. All the directors said no. If I'd stayed in the box, *Spider* would never have been made.

Look at a situation from all angles. If you're a visual person, try drawing a circle or a flow chart of what you're doing. Then draw other flow charts to show other ways of getting it done. Leaders see alternatives immediately, because alternatives prevent failure from setting in. It's like Alice in Wonderland not being able to fit through the door. There's always another door; find it, then take a chance and go through that door. I guarantee you will go a step further. New approaches reveal new opportunities, or new people, or something that will aid you in furthering your conquest. That's how nature works. If you take the shot and trust in yourself, you won't fail. It's never too late to latch onto something new.

Everything is a test. Even if you quit your job to pursue a dream and think you've just made a serious mistake, see it as a test. Have faith in yourself that you'll find a way through the situation if you're creative enough. I've had suicidal thoughts. I've had a breakdown. I turned off my phone, packed my bags and drove away. I drove up north without a clue where I was going. I ended up in a small town just as winter was ending. Phil Kent heard I was in trouble and called me. When I told him I was going away, he said, "Before you go kill yourself, stop by a bookstore and get this book: *Buck Up, Suck Up and Come Back When You Foul Up*. Written by James Carville and Paul Begala from CNN, it's an amazing book about the many times they've screwed up and come back to face the music. The most serious incident was on the Clinton campaign trail when they reported that he'd never had an affair and it turned out he had. Carville and Begala endured the embarrassment by keeping their eyes on the ball. "It's about the economy," they kept insisting. As long as they focused on that, nothing else mattered. If somebody tried to bring them down with gossip, they'd hit back with the economy. As long as you focus on the one thing you want, nothing else matters.

Focus on the goal

A friend of mine decided to leave a successful career as an editor to become a producer and make a film with another friend. He went with the wrong person and the whole thing fell apart. He's had a few successes, though. He's made out a cheque for $1-million that he keeps on his fridge and he says he's going to cash it. When he told me that, I said, "That's great, but here's the problem. It's on your fridge covered with coupons and magnets. Put it on your bedroom ceiling where you'll see it every night before going to sleep."

Now, he's close to accomplishing his goal, close to that one million, he's feeling good about himself and he's got a great relationship. Focus on the goal, not the garbage. Keep your eye on the ball. Your journey is your own. Other people may achieve successes before you do; as hard as it is, be happy for them, rather than feeling that you're competing with them. Your happiness for their success will help give you peace of mind, allowing you to stay focused.

Many people have passed me. Actors routinely see other actors with a similar look and maybe less talent get jobs they've been passed over for. Brendan Fehr, my close friend and business partner, says, "It's not a race, it's a marathon." How true. But if you find you want to trip the runner next to you, don't do it.

Every night, I say, "Universe, bring me the people I need to go to the next level. Bring me the situation I need. Do it in a way that I know it occurred from the exercise." I tried it with a stand-up comic and she got a call offering her a part the next morning. A logical person may be sceptical, but I'd challenge that person to try it. Every time I use this approach, something happens. It's always undeniable that it happened because I requested it. It keeps me motivated when things happen the way I want them to.

I return e-mails and phone calls between five-thirty and six in the morning. Everything gets done first thing. I have that serene time to myself. For me, a typical day is about getting as much accomplished as early as possible. According to Robert Greene, the trick is to make it look easy. I make it look so easy that many people think I don't work at all. If you want to go to lunch, I can go to lunch with you and spend an hour-and-a-half talking and laughing. When everybody's rushing back to work, I'm meandering, enjoying the day. I have so many jobs and companies that nobody knows what I do. I purposefully make it look easy and that's part of the illusion. When people come to one of my events, it's so completely different that they don't know what to say. For me, getting up early is a great way to go. Mark Breslin is up late at night, networking at parties until two or three in the morning. Then he starts his day late. To each to his own.

Seize opportunities without worrying about the details

I never look at what I need to seize an opportunity. My philosophy is to seize the opportunity and have faith that what I need to bring it to fruition will come to me. It's that simple. Don't worry about the details! Grab the opportunity and the details will work themselves out. It requires having faith in yourself and the universe.

Many times I've pursued a deal, a potential client, or an opportunity with no idea of how I'm going to pay for it or pull the resources together. But I don't worry about it.

Recently, I tried to get Dr. John Demartini to sign with BurmanBooks. He'd starred in the movie *The Secret* and had been on *Larry King Live* the previous week. I was nervous because he was in such high demand. I was certain another publisher would make him a better offer or that he'd just see us as too small.

The reality was that we were so small, I couldn't afford to pay the long-distance phone bill and still retain enough money to publish his book! My biggest problem was finding a phone to make our scheduled long-distance call. My cell phone would have to do, even though I hate using a cell phone for important calls, in case it drops the call or there's static. However, I had no choice. I used my cell phone and sat beside the window hoping for a stronger signal.

Picture me sitting on the window ledge holding a cell phone to my ear and cupping the mouthpiece to block out the ambient traffic noise, telling Dr. Demartini of the big plans I had for him. I spoke with my eyes closed, visualizing the book in front of me. I spoke with passion and most importantly, I believed in myself strongly enough to know that I would attract what I'd need as it was needed.

Obviously Dr. Demartini believed in my vision as well, since he signed with us three hours later. If the worst happened and I couldn't fulfil my obligation to him, he could walk away at any time. *But* it's better to at least try for the home run, than not go to bat at all.

Dream big

Mark Breslin: One thing that I have to say about Sanjay is that he doesn't think small. He thinks very big. He often comes to me with huge, multi-multi-multi-million-dollar deals. I'm more of a practical, day-to-day guy. I built my business up from scratch. I collected enough pennies that they finally became nickels and the nickels finally became quarters and the quarters finally became dollars. He tries to put huge things together. The deals all make sense, but I don't think he has the experience to convince somebody to put down that kind of money. I'm always trying to get him to think smaller, but thinking big is a sign of the entrepreneur.

I always dream big. I don't believe in "realistic" goals. Every book on negotiation teaches you to go for more than you think you'll get and allow yourself to be reduced down to what you actually can get. Always dream the biggest dream. I don't think I would've been the producer of a Cronenberg movie at the age of twenty-three if I didn't dream big. You might have to swing the bat a lot of times, but sooner or later, you'll hit one out of the park.

At one point, Tyler Perry, writer and producer of *Madea's Family Reunion,* was living out of a box. Seven years later, he was worth over $60-million. He wrote a play that became a movie that became a franchise. How? He didn't give up on his dream and didn't settle for anything less, even when things were at their worst.

Sydnee: Sanjay seems to allow the fairies of the universe, as I call them, to do his bidding for him. He just says, "I want to do this," and then he lets it happen.

Vanessa: He's genuinely interested in encouraging me and giving advice. Many people in the industry don't offer the extra hand and say, 'this is where you're at and this is where you need to be.' That's something I get from Sanjay. I meet a lot of people who are just talk. He's given me sound, grounded advice. He said I have to build my resume, to taste my own blood. I loved that. It's tough in the entertainment industry. There's always competition and it's about meeting people and getting exposure. There are many beautiful, talented people with perhaps a better agent or better contacts. At the end of the day, you have to pay your dues. You have to get out there and give an arm and a leg and pursue your dreams. It won't be a diamond on a silver platter. There are hundreds of thousands of people who think they can make it. Tasting your own blood is like saying you've got to toil and sweat and bleed a little to get to where you want to go. It isn't about going against your morals or beliefs. You just really have to work for it. The more you work for it, the more people you meet, the more productions you're in. Even if you're working for free, the movie could go to a festival or a producer's hands. People start talking. When I went to my current agent and said I'm doing independent productions, he looked at me and said, "Why are you doing those things?" But I've got to do it, because he's not getting me auditions. If I'm going to further my career, it has to be me who does it, not him. It was great advice on Sanjay's part.

I've had a lot of training and I've been ready for a while to go to the next level with my auditions and see the right people, but unfortunately it just hasn't been happening. I can't just sit at home and cry, asking myself, "Why me? Life isn't fair." I've got to put that aside, look at it and say, "If this is what I want to do for the rest of my life, if this is my passion and if this is what my heart's telling me to do, I've got to put everything else aside. At this point, it's about the acting, the craft. Even if there are things that maybe won't give me money, I'll do them.

EXERCISE: Dream Big

People always have daydreams, but they may not realize that visualization works. Look at Anthony Robbins! I've had first-hand experience of conversations I've visualized actually happening, of my dreams coming true. Visualization is a great way to keep yourself motivated and energized to take the next step. In my experience, two out of three times it happens exactly the way I've visualized it. The other three times, although it doesn't happen the way I thought it would, I still accomplish my goal.

Start with small, simple wishes. Try it with something like receiving money. Don't get caught up in the 'how' or 'when', just focus on money coming into your hands. See it, feel it and experience it. Watch how quickly it happens! You'll be amazed.

Be conscious of the way you visualize your dream. For instance, if you want to be a successful actor, but only see yourself as wealthy and holding an Oscar, your underlying goal is simply ego gratification that has nothing to do with acting. Instead, try visualizing every step along the way; how you got there, who you worked with, what type of movie you're winning the Oscar for. Visualize every detail. Once you can see the details clearly, you know it's a passion and a solid goal that you can achieve.

What do you want out of life? Don't worry about whether it's 'realistic.' Think about your dream in specific detail. Picture yourself there, doing what you dream of doing or speaking to the person you want to approach. Now really feel it. Get emotionally involved. Send out the energy that you're really passionate about making your dream happen. Your subconscious mind doesn't know what's real and what's not. If you can convince yourself that you're accomplishing your goals, little by little, you actually will.

Chapter 10:

Endear Yourself to Others

Phil Kent, chairman of Turner Broadcasting, has become like an older brother to me. Turner Broadcasting runs twenty-five different stations plus the Atlanta Braves and other ventures; $6-billion goes through his company annually. But there isn't a moment I can't call him and say, "I'm in trouble. I have to negotiate this deal. Where can I go with it?" or "Can you look at this and give me your advice?" I don't know if everyone can do this, but it came from having a personal relationship with him. Subconsciously, I bond myself to my mentors. We actually feel an emotional connection.

People are attracted to positive energy

It begins by feeling good about yourself. Feel good, look good and you'll automatically start to resonate that. Start with something you look great in. For me, it's suits. When I put on my best suit, best shirt and best tie, I look good and feel great and then I exude confidence. Even though the suit itself can't give you confidence, if you believe it's giving you confidence, it will. The suit triggers confidence to manifest. Also, make sure that you're relaxed. When you're relaxed, you don't care whether people are noticing you. When you enter a room with a relaxed attitude, people look at you. It happens even when I walk into a mall wearing sweats. I feel good because I just worked out or brought a deal together, but people do a double-take. They aren't doing it because they think I'm good looking; they're doing it because there's an energy coming from me that they're attracted to. People are attracted to positive energy.

One mistake people make is asking, "Why would this person want to meet with me? I'm not big enough or good enough." Always put yourself in the position of that person. What's in it for them? If you walk in offering them something, it's more intriguing for them to sit back and listen. The more they like you, the more time they'll give you.

Debbie Nightingale didn't take in the fourteen-year-old puppy just because she was nice and had time to spend answering my questions and showing me the ropes. No! It was a trade. She got a person to run the small errands that needed to be run, but take time away from more important things. I never got paid; I learned. Instead of money, I earned wisdom. It's a concept that I use daily.

> *Debbie Nightingale:* He's soaked up everything, from me and anybody. I was happy to feed it to him. When I see somebody who's excited about something, I'm happy to help them push forward as far as they can go. I loved that. If I can help him out, I'm happy to do that.

Before walking into a meeting, I visualize the conversation, what we'll talk about, how they'll react, what the result will be and their body language. I'll picture everything. When I walk in, I'm usually a little nervous, but I already have an image of what I want to achieve. Visualizing it makes me feel more secure; it's already been played out. People will tell you exactly what they're looking for, what they want and what their feelings are if you'll just shut up and listen. The more you listen, the more they'll talk, because most people are uncomfortable with silence. Everything you need to know about how to make a deal happen will be apparent in the first three minutes.

You can learn a lot about somebody's personality by looking around their office or home and commenting on what you see. For instance, if you see a mounted sword, you could say, "That's a great sword." They might respond, "I was in Scotland and I loved *Braveheart*, so I picked it up." Now you know they're into conflict and aggressiveness. The more aggressive you are, the more he'll respect you. He's given you that information.

Sydnee: Sanjay likes to make people feel comfortable. When we first met, we went to dinner. I ordered wine and so did he. I later found out that Sanjay doesn't drink alcohol! I asked him about it and he said that he'd learned or felt throughout his life that it was polite not to let a lady drink alone. I kind of laughed and thought, well, he's right. That does offer a kind of comfort when I'm having a drink.

Don't be afraid of influential people

I needed a Dodge Viper to shoot a music video. Who'd lend me one for the weekend? It's a $200,000 vehicle. I called the president of Chrysler, the late Yves Landry and he called me back. I told him I was shooting a video out of my pocket and trying to succeed as a video director. He said he'd ship me one in three days. Then I told him, "I don't have three days. I only have one." Then he said, "I'll make some phone calls for you." The president of Chrysler was making phone calls for me! He couldn't make the schedule work, so that didn't happen. (I stayed in touch with him for a while, though. He'd laugh at some of my adventures and offer advice. He died a few years later.) When the Viper didn't work out, I called the Vice President of Porsche. Not only did he provide one, he even drove it in the video.

Tom Cruise was a big shareholder in a children's newspaper called *Tomorrow's Morning*. It wasn't going anywhere and I thought I could get it moving forward; then Tom Cruise would owe me a favour. I called Adam Winter, who'd started the paper and we negotiated that we'd split the Canadian and European rights. I called Bernie Wilson, the senior partner of PriceWaterhouseCoopers and I asked, "Do you want to do this? Tom Cruise would be in on it." He loved it. We met with the presidents of Canada's largest newspapers and we sold it to one of them, but he eventually left to manage a baseball team. Even though the deal died, I made some great contacts during that deal.

Don't be afraid of influential people. If you ask for something they can deliver, most will not only help you, but they'll do so gladly. I can't stress that enough.

EXERCISE: Networking

At your next function, make it your goal to walk out with five new business cards. Do it in a way that makes people say, "I look forward to your call." If you keep saying to people, "Give me your card," you're being a nag and you should be selling for Amway. Instead, do it in a way that's subtle, a way that makes them offer you their card. You're making them like you by establishing a rapport. That's the key to networking. This exercise will help you understand how energy works.

If you really want to challenge yourself, do this exercise every day. At first, you might feel shy or make others feel standoffish. After some practice, you'll be able to do it very easily. This provides you with a model for how to deal with people, influential or not. It doesn't matter whether or not we're successful; "In the end, we all have to wipe our asses before we get off the toilet," as Redd Foxx said.

Chapter 11:

What to Do When Someone Says Yes!

After spending so much time pursuing a goal and trying to find the opportunity you want, when somebody finally does write you a cheque or give you the opportunity, you may panic. Not everybody does, but I sure do. I think to myself, *Oh my God, I've hyped my abilities and interest so much. What if I can't deliver?*

Recently, I pitched a current affairs show to CBC's Newsworld. After having spoken to them both, I said I had two big-name attorneys on board; one a criminal defence lawyer and the other a civil libertarian. Both love the spotlight, they've reached the pinnacles of their careers and are known for having conflicting opinions. Unfortunately, when I spoke to the lawyers again to seal the deal, it didn't work out. They posed hurdles with scheduling and subject matter and the negotiations fell apart.

What could I do? The opportunity was in hand and the Head of Programming, Heaton Dyer, had already scheduled a meeting with me. I didn't want to admit defeat, so instead I said I had another concept that was just as good, but these two people would pose even more conflict on camera. I didn't give away much information about what had happened, nor did I let on that I hadn't been able to deliver. I framed it in such a way that it sounded like I'd intentionally made the change to increase viewership.

Now, Heaton is no dummy. He didn't reach his position by being fooled. However, anybody who gives you an opportunity probably started from scratch themselves. If your plans don't work out the way you want them to, those people are likely to understand what you're going through. Some of their plans haven't worked out either. Heaton didn't pull the plug, or focus on my failure to deliver the initial concept. He simply sat, heard me out and thought about the new concept for about a minute. Then he stood up and said, "Sign them and come back."

I found two other people who could fill the spots, secured the deal and arranged to pitch it to CBC again. Amazingly, one of them still pulled out at the last minute. Now I was sure I was in trouble. I went back to Heaton exuding all the confidence in the world, while squirming inside because I thought they'd kill the deal. I said the show would be even better with the two new people; one of whom I now had to replace.

Eventually, we got a great show that did well in the ratings and the debate, according to Heaton, was 'above expectation.' He knew full well the ups and downs I was experiencing. He stuck with me not because I had pitched a show that would revolutionize programming on CBC, but because he saw talent and persistence. What I didn't realize until later was that Heaton wouldn't have pulled the plug because he wasn't betting on the show; he was betting on me!

I can't think of myself ever accepting defeat or trying to get every detail finalized before moving forward. I jump straight to step three, because I'm certain that steps one and two will fall into place once I've made step three. That works for everybody. Be versatile with steps one and two. If you run into a road-block down one avenue, switch to another right away. Don't hesitate or second-guess yourself. Just go. If you pitch a great show to a broadcaster and tell them high-calibre people will be involved, getting those people will come naturally. But you need to believe in yourself and that it will work out.

If you swing the bat enough times, eventually you'll hit the ball. Don't be afraid that you won't be able to run the bases. You will. The people giving you the opportunity will probably help you if you run into problems, as long as they see you're still trying. They're not giving you the opportunity to see you fail. They're giving you the opportunity because they believe in you and believe you'll make them even more successful. *They're on your side.*

Once, I was asked to run a political fundraiser. At first I dismissed it by saying I don't get involved in politics. After a few months, I couldn't stop thinking about it. I made an excuse to turn it down, when really I was afraid I'd fail. Even though I'd never run a fundraiser before and had no team to back me up, I accepted. But I knew that because step three was already there, steps one and two would work themselves out. I went to the best publicists and event planners I know and asked for help. They all said yes, and overnight I had my team. After the first meeting, everything went into fifth gear.

What we don't always realize is that the people coming to us believe we have potential and talent. They wouldn't ask for our assistance if they didn't think we had what it takes. They have faith in us. Have faith in yourself, even if you're scared and unsure about whether you can pull it off. It's just your fear of failure or success talking. Relax and go forward. You have what it takes, or you wouldn't have been asked. If you're afraid, admit it! It's okay. Only our egos stop us from admitting our fears. Once you admit to your fear, you'll find you have even *more* support to help you find a solution.

When I told a former agent at CAA about the CBC show, I predicted it would be a complete disaster. Then he told me a story about a job he'd done when he was still an agent, putting together a concert in Central Park with Diana Ross. He thought the rain insurance was too expensive, so he cancelled it. On the day of the concert, there was a torrential rainfall. Diana Ross was on stage surrounded by electrical equipment, singing to a packed Central Park and it was raining cats and dogs. He was watching her, thinking his career was over, as each raindrop fell. As it turned out, the rain actually made it one of Diana Ross' most memorable television appearances.

The next day at the office, his boss asked if he'd learned from the experience. He said yes. His boss replied, "Good. Move on." He didn't lose his job. It was never talked about again and his career continued to evolve until he became what he is today, the Chairman of a large media corporation.

Every successful person has encountered a situation in which they've had an opportunity and then second-guessed it. In his biography, Michael Eisner writes about walking on the Disney lot wondering how on earth he was going to run such a massive company. Jack Welch, one of the best CEOs of all time, wrote about GE having so many divisions and products, he'd never be able to keep up and know what was going on in them all.

If you're frightened of success, you're not alone. In fact, you're in good company. Be strong and move forward. Remember that the people around you want you to succeed. They chose you because you're good enough to put steps one and two together and have the persistence to see the job through to completion.

Now, make today the first day of your new life! Go out and seize your right to live the life you want to live. No dream is too big. If you have persistence, it will be yours.

FEAR JOURNAL

I'm going to show you how fear can either stop you from attaining something or help you understand yourself and your abilities. The choice will be yours.

Everyday you will write down what you did that scared you, what the results were and why you were scared of it in the first place. You will do this for 10 days. If you really are serious about your success, then you will commit to yourself for 10 days. Be specific. The more specific you are, the more you will get out of this. The less interest you take in yourself, the less progression you will see.

Day 1

What I did that scared me today

_____

_____

_____

_____

_____

What were the results?

_____

_____

_____

_____

_____

Why was I scared in the first place?

_____

_____

_____

_____

_____

Day 2

What I did that scared me today:

_____

_____

_____

_____

_____

What were the results?

_____

_____

_____

_____

_____

Why was I scared in the first place?

_____

_____

_____

_____

_____

Day 3

What I did that scared me today:

_____

_____

_____

_____

_____

What were the results?

_____

_____

_____

_____

_____

Why was I scared in the first place?

_____

_____

_____

_____

_____

Day 4

What I did that scared me today:

_____

_____

_____

_____

_____

What were the results?

_____

_____

_____

_____

_____

Why was I scared in the first place?

_____

_____

_____

_____

Day 5

What I did that scared me today:

_____

_____

_____

_____

_____

What were the results?

_____

_____

_____

_____

_____

Why was I scared in the first place?

_____

_____

_____

_____

_____

Day 6

What I did that scared me today:

_____

_____

_____

_____

_____

What were the results?

_____

_____

_____

_____

_____

Why was I scared in the first place?

_____

_____

_____

_____

_____

Day 7

What I did that scared me today:

_____

_____

_____

_____

_____

What were the results?

_____

_____

_____

_____

_____

Why was I scared in the first place?

_____

_____

_____

_____

_____

Day 8

What I did that scared me today:

_____

_____

_____

_____

_____

What were the results?

_____

_____

_____

_____

_____

Why was I scared in the first place?

_____

_____

_____

_____

Day 9

What I did that scared me today:

_____

_____

_____

_____

_____

What were the results?

_____

_____

_____

_____

_____

Why was I scared in the first place?

_____

_____

_____

_____

_____

Day 10

What I did that scared me today:

_____

_____

_____

_____

_____

What were the results?

_____

_____

_____

_____

_____

Why was I scared in the first place?

_____

_____

_____

_____

_____